PSYCHOTHERAPY WITH MALE SURVIVORS OF SEXUAL ABUSE

FORENSIC PSYCHOTHERAPY MONOGRAPH SERIES

Series Editor: Professor Brett Kahr
Honorary Consultant: Dr Estela V. Welldon

Other titles in the Series

Violence: A Public Health Menace and a Public Health Approach
Edited by Sandra L. Bloom

Life Within Hidden Worlds: Psychotherapy in Prisons
Edited by Jessica Williams Saunders

Forensic Psychotherapy and Psychopathology: Winnicottian Perspectives
Edited by Brett Kahr

Dangerous Patients: A Psychodynamic Approach to Risk Assessment and Management
Edited by Ronald Doctor

Anxiety at 35,000 Feet: An Introduction to Clinical Aerospace Psychology
Robert Bor

The Mind of the Paedophile: Psychoanalytic Perspectives
Edited by Charles W. Socarides

Violent Adolescents: Understanding the Destructive Impulse
Edited by Lynn Greenwood

Violence in Children: Understanding and Helping Those Who Harm
Edited by Rosemary Campher

Murder: A Psychotherapeutic Investigation
Edited by Ronald Doctor

Psychic Assaults and Frightened Clinicians: Countertransference in Forensic Settings
Edited by John Gordon and Gabriel Kirtchuk

Forensic Aspects of Dissociative Identity Disorder
Edited by Adah Sachs and Graeme Galton

Playing with Dynamite: A Personal Approach to the Psychoanalytic Understanding of Perversions, Violence, and Criminality
Estela V. Welldon

The Internal World of the Juvenile Sex Offender: Through a Glass Darkly then Face to Face
Timothy Keogh

Disabling Perversions: Forensic Psychotherapy with People with Intellectual Disabilities
Alan Corbett

Sexual Abuse and the Sexual Offender: Common Man or Monster?
Barry Maletzky

PSYCHOTHERAPY WITH MALE SURVIVORS OF SEXUAL ABUSE

The Invisible Men

Alan Corbett

Routledge
Taylor & Francis Group
LONDON AND NEW YORK

First published 2016 by Karnac Books Ltd.

2 Park Square, Milton Park, Abingdon, Oxfordshire OX14 4RN
52 Vanderbilt Avenue, New York, NY 10017

Routledge is an imprint of the Taylor & Francis Group, an informa business

First issued in hardback 2019

British Library Cataloguing in Publication Data

A C.I.P. for this book is available from the British Library

ISBN-13: 978-1-78220-196-0 (pbk)
ISBN-13: 978-0-367-32494-0 (hbk)

Typeset by V Publishing Solutions Pvt Ltd., Chennai, India

To Pete, an expert in the art of resilience, survival, and hope

CONTENTS

ACKNOWLEDGEMENTS

I am pleased to contribute another volume to the Forensic Psychotherapy Monograph Series, largely because it means working with Professor Brett Kahr, the kindest and most supportive editor and friend. It also involves collaborating with the wonderful team at Karnac, all of whom work tirelessly to make the production process as painless as possible. Illness struck just as I started writing this book, and my thanks are inevitably shaped by this. I am therefore acknowledging not only the professional support of colleagues, but the care of friends and family who, without realising it, helped me write this book by helping me get well. I was truly delighted to discover that the overlap between colleagues and friends was far bigger than I ever imagined.

Special thanks to P. J. and Trina Corbett, Kathy Whelan, Aida Smith, Pete Loye, Tamsin Cottis, Dr Noelle Blackman, Helen McCormack, Patricia Day, Isabel Montero, Daniel Linehan, Dr Anne Alvarez, Dr Valerie Sinason, Dr Estela Welldon, Tom and Phyllis Cooke, Georgina Hoare, Sally Anderson, Mary Eleftheriou, Marios Andreou, Joanna Griffin, Sarah Van Gogh, Alex Duffield, David Richardson, Ken Clarke, Peter Chapman, Elton Jackson, Michael May, Cathy Yexley, Brendan Thornton, Brian Horgan, Gregory Curran, Cary Yageman, Monalee Prange Humesky, Anthony Schulist, Claire Harris, Dr Eimir

McGrath, and Mary Hogan. Some helped inform my clinical thinking, some helped me get well enough to write through acts of kindness, and many did both.

I am grateful to my colleagues at the various organisations of which I am part, especially Respond, Dr Hilary Dodson and the Guild of Psychotherapists Training Committee, Dr Georgina Parkes and the Institute for Psychotherapy and Disability, Dr Rachel Thomas and the Clinic for Dissociative Studies, and all at the CARI Foundation and ICAP (Immigrant Counselling and Psychotherapy). I am particularly grateful to my colleagues at Survivors UK, and to Richard Curen for initially introducing me to them. All these organisations have had a profound impact upon my clinical development. The most important and least visible co-creators of this book are my patients and supervisees who have taught me an astonishing amount about resilience, thoughtfulness, and creativity. As with all I do, this book could not have been written without the support and love of my husband Peter McKeown.

ABOUT THE AUTHOR

Alan Corbett is the editor of the Institute of Psychotherapy and Disability Monograph Series, and the author of a number of books, chapters, and papers on aspects of working psychoanalytically with trauma, abuse, and disability. He has been Clinical Director of Respond, ICAP, and the CARI Foundation, and is a member of the training committee of the Guild of Psychotherapists. He is also a psychotherapist and supervisor in private practice.

SERIES EDITOR'S FOREWORD

Brett Kahr

Not long ago, while seated in the back of a London taxi, a BBC news item blared forth from the driver's radio, announcing that a case had just gone to trial in the courts concerning a man who claimed that his wife had raped him. Upon hearing this, the rather incredulous taxi driver began to scoff: "Jesus Christ, what sort of man would let his wife do that to him? Besides, you can't rape a man". Clearly distressed by this report, the driver then tried to engage me in conversation, asking, "You don't believe that, do you, guv? You don't believe that men can be raped by *women*, do you?" He then chortled and admitted, "Gosh, if my wife raped me, I'd be only too thrilled!"

Exhausted from a long day at work, I did not particularly relish the prospect of having to convince this person that both women *and* men can become victims of sexual violence. Nevertheless, I offered some sort of explanation by way of reply, although I believe that I failed to convince the driver that the BBC news story might well be credible.

If I should ever meet this London taxi driver again—which does happen from time to time, even in a big city such as this one—I would now be able to proclaim proudly, "If you still have doubts that male sexual abuse actually exists, let me send you a copy of Dr Alan Corbett's new book, *Psychotherapy with Male Survivors of Sexual Abuse: The Invisible Men*. That will settle the matter entirely."

As we know only too well, sexual violence causes untold devastation to the body, to the mind, and to the soul. And its victims—or survivors—include girls and boys, as well as women and men, who will often suffer, in consequence, from severe psychopathology and from psychosomatic illnesses.

During my own lifetime, the mental health profession has made enormous strides in the recognition of sexual abuse, and many of the titles published in our Karnac Books Forensic Psychotherapy Monograph Series have contributed knowledge to this very field of study. But we still have much more to learn.

Fortunately, in the ongoing struggle against sexual abuse and other forms of violence, it gives me great pleasure to present Alan Corbett's latest publication, which I regard as one of the most important engagements with the topic of sexual cruelty towards men currently in print.

Dr Corbett will be well known to readers of our forensic psychotherapy monographs as a highly respected and much admired clinician, teacher, and writer within the mental health field. His previous book, *Disabling Perversions: Forensic Psychotherapy with People with Intellectual Disabilities*, remains the gold standard textbook about forensic disability psychotherapy—a field that Corbett has pioneered—and now, his new book on "invisible men" will come to occupy a similar position among studies on male sexual abuse.

As a psychotherapist, Alan Corbett has had the unique opportunity to hear horrific narratives of abuse from his patients—both male and female—over many decades. And although this work must remain confidential, Corbett has, nevertheless, found a way to convey the truth and the impact of these revelations of abuse while still protecting the privacy of those who have entrusted him with their deepest confessions and secrets and terrors. As Corbett explains in his beautifully poetic prose, "Psychotherapy tends to be written in invisible ink." Thankfully, he has found a way to preserve the integrity of these narratives and to help the invisible ink become legible so that we may all learn from what his patients have told him and from what he has processed and digested of these awful experiences.

In the Introduction, Corbett explains, quite chillingly, that nowadays, sexual abuse remains a massive global problem, facilitated, alas, by the wonders of modern technology. Perpetrators of sexual violence can now target vulnerable people through the internet, and consequently, abuse remains merely a click away. Fortunately, as we all become better educated about the realities of abuse, such awareness will, we hope, contribute to its ultimate eradication. But this will not be an easy battle to fight, as Corbett reminds us, owing to the tragic reality that many survivors of abuse will themselves become perpetrators as a result of the pain that they have endured and the fury that such molestation has engendered. From the very outset, Corbett, steeped in the forensic perspective, reminds us that we must not create unhelpful splits between victims and perpetrators. By contrast, we must remember that every perpetrator began life as a victim, and that every victim has the capacity to perpetrate likewise.

After providing us with a skilfully crafted introduction, Dr Corbett then offers us eleven gracefully written chapters which, collectively, provide a truly wise and comprehensive landscape of the field of sexual abuse studies, focusing on the abuse of boys and men, as well as on the challenging art of psychotherapeutic treatment. With great boldness and clinical honesty, Corbett presents a blunt and realistic portrait of the world of sexual abuse, reminding us that anyone can suffer from such attacks, regardless of age, sexual orientation, or setting. A male—whether young or old, heterosexual or homosexual—can be raped in a nursery, in a school, or in church, as well as in prison, on the battlefield, or even in the privacy of one's own home. And the consequences will invariably be devastating, so much so that Corbett questions whether the dignified term "survivor"—though hard-won by campaigners and activists and mental health workers alike—becomes a euphemism for the victimhood which trails many men throughout the whole of their lives.

On the basis of his clinical work and, also his supervisory work, Corbett knows only too well that many of those who have experienced rape—especially those deprived of opportunities for psychotherapy—will suffer from lifelong psychopathological consequences, including a much higher tendency towards migraine—an important, but perhaps unsurprising, finding in view of the fact that many survivors have often experienced penetration not only of one or more bodily orifices, but also of the mind. Corbett has worked with many abused and traumatised men who yearn for destruction and even death, and who appear wraith-like, as though drained of all vitality.

Throughout each chapter, Corbett provides not only chilling and illuminating clinical case material, but also well-considered theoretical explications of the various obstacles and challenges to the mind of the male abuse victim or survivor. Corbett elucidates his concept of "toxic masculinity", explaining that the act of being penetrated—though potentially brutal for either sex—presents particular psychological challenges to the male who has grown up with a fantasy of being inviolable. Indeed, in the mind of many pre-heterosexual boys who fantasise about penetrating a girlfriend or wife in years to come, they become the *architects* of penetration, not its *recipients*. Thus, when this aspect of masculinity becomes challenged by sexual abuse, any penetrative assault will shatter the boy's concept of his own sense of maleness in quite a profound way.

Drawing upon his extensive knowledge of psychoanalysis, Corbett does not adopt a simple, monolithic model of traumatisation. Although he certainly appreciates the grotesque consequences of molestation, Corbett has recognised that a particular act or acts of sexual abuse may not necessarily be the most pathogenic experiences in the biography of a victim. Rather, as Corbett has demonstrated, sexual violence can often serve to inflame or exacerbate earlier injuries to the mind and to the sense of self, owing to the fact that many patients will already have internalised perverse family structures. Indeed, when one has experienced parental hatred during the earliest years of life, not to mention abandonment, neglect, impingements, or lack of basic mirroring in the nexus of the baby-caregiver relationship, then any subsequent experience of bodily abuse in later years will become that much more devastating.

In his demystification of the realms of the sexual abuse of males, Corbett does not write in euphemisms. With both a compassionate and forthright manner, he reveals the dangerous sequelae from which many victims will suffer, including the potentiality to become embroiled in a world of anonymous sex and chemsex with multiple partners, in search of thrills—a manic defence designed to soothe pain. Corbett, however, has observed that the excitement of such sexual encounters might be described more accurately as "pseudo-excitement", and that the participants in such activities often miss out on the true possibilities of intimacy and connectedness so necessary for solid mental health. Corbett has highlighted the tragic reality that for many survivors of abuse, "the notion of an ordinary, reciprocal, non-traumatic sexual encounter" simply does not exist.

Dr Corbett's book brims with important technical considerations, too numerous to itemise in a brief foreword, but each a gem, based on copious clinical experience. For instance, Corbett rightly cautions colleagues that in working with sexually compulsive men, one must be very careful not to release them from their addictions too quickly or too intrusively. As Corbett explains, "Our attempts to wean them off their compulsion will be experienced as a form of attack, touching on early experiences of deprivation." Thus, with wisdom, he has observed that for those men who participate in compulsive sexual rituals, the "horror show" may also be experienced as something "exciting" and "colourful", and therefore, symptoms must be mourned gradually and must not be ripped away, however destructive these behaviours may seem to the clinician.

In a similar vein, Alan Corbett has written about the judiciousness with which the mental health professional must consider whether to work with the traditional analytical couch or whether one should, by contrast, use ordinary chairs. In one case, Corbett opted for chairs, rather than for the divan, fearful that by inviting the patient to adopt a prone position, he might "sever any potential connection between us both". This remains a topic of considerable interest and importance for contemporary psychoanalytical clinicians, and it pleases me that Corbett has highlighted this as a matter for further collegial discussion and consideration.

Corbett's refreshingly honest observations will bring relief to fellow practitioners who have struggled with the countertransferential burdens of treating highly distressed and even damaged abuse victims who unburden themselves and who then drop out of treatment, projecting all of their traumatic feelings of shame and failure into the clinician. Sometimes psychotherapists will really suffer at the hands of patients who treat us in a deeply denigratory manner, re-enacting the abuse in the context of the transference. Thus, of his work with a man called Nawaz, Corbett writes, "I had to conclude that the intimacy of our sessions was too much for him to bear. In truth, it was too much for me to bear as well." Rarely does a mental health clinician speak in such a blunt manner about some of the awful struggles that we must all endure when working in the arena of severe psychopathology.

I cannot conclude my remarks about *Psychotherapy with Male Survivors of Sexual Abuse: The Invisible Men* without mentioning that Corbett writes prose with marvellous grace and with tremendous literary sensibility. Consequently, readers will enjoy the experience of savouring each well-structured chapter and, often, each stunningly crafted sentence—such a refreshing contrast to some of the very stodgy writing which mental health practitioners must often contend. Not only has Corbett penned his text in a splendid manner, but he has done so in a scholarly style as well, synthesising an enormous amount of highly pertinent professional literature from a wide variety of disciplines. Whereas much contemporary psychoanalytical writing draws upon the "usual suspects", such as Wilfred Bion, Melanie Klein, and Herbert Rosenfeld, Corbett's book brims with a far greater breadth of well-integrated references from both classical psychoanalysis as well as contemporary psychoanalysis; additionally, he has cited much of the American literature as well as the British contributions. But even more so, he has most usefully incorporated many of the important research findings from the fields of psychiatry, clinical psychology, psychopathology, psychosomatics, health psychology, sexology, and sexual health, to boot, thus providing us with a true education in the arena of traumatology.

It pleases me immensely to invite readers to embrace Dr Corbett's latest work, which I regard as a substantial contribution to human psychology, and I thank him for his generosity in sharing such hard-earned work in such a lucid, compassionate, helpful, and hopeful manner. I have every confidence that this book will remain of immense value for a very long time to come.

Professor Brett Kahr
Series Editor
Forensic Psychotherapy Monograph Series
London

INTRODUCTION

Invisibility is the motif of this book, and in writing it I came to recognise that creating a book is an exercise in rendering visible work that is usually hidden far from the gaze of others. Psychotherapy tends to be written in invisible ink, and it is mainly through the writing of clinical stories that this complex but simple process of psychic relief being provided through the telling of a story can be decoded and shared. Writing is also an exercise in hope. The writer hopes more than anything that the book will make sense to someone other than himself. Writing is an insular, solitary occupation in which we hope to make a connection with an imagined reader. I hope also that the heart of this kind of clinically based book—the stories of the men with whom I have worked—will be treated with respect and understanding. I have disguised every story to the point of near invisibility in the knowledge that any patient reading the clinical accounts herein will fail to recognise himself, but will recognise some of the core experiences that populate the histories and treatments of men who have been sexually abused.

I wrote this book because for some time I had longed for a contemporary examination of the experiences of men who had been sexually abused, as revealed in the consulting room. My work with male survivors had been influenced by the writing of such clinicians as Lew (1988),

Mendel (1995), Gartner (1999), and Scarce (2001), and for some years I had been aware of a growing divergence between theory and practice. The classical psychoanalytic bedrock of our encounters with sexual trauma remains the work of Freud and his followers, and the clinical foundations of this book are built on the legacy of object-relational thinking, an approach I have found particularly helpful in understanding the interface between sexual trauma and the formation of the self. There was, however, a growing lacuna in the literature. More men are daring to enter the consulting room and are daring further to bring in aspects of their pain that were rarely spoken of twenty years ago, let alone a century before. Sexual trauma and its impact on all aspects of the psyche have not changed in quality or impact. What has changed is the context in which abuse can occur, the means by which rape can be facilitated and, crucially, the meaning of being a man in the early part of the twenty-first century.

Rape can now be facilitated through social media. It is not just sexual partners that are a click away; perpetrators of abuse are adept at perverting the aims of sites such as Tinder and Grindr. These sites can also become a powerfully embedded part of a victim's defence mechanism, providing him with a socially sanctioned hiding place for his post-traumatic sexual compulsions. Assaults are facilitated through the use of devastating drugs that render the victim powerless and amnesiac. Relatives of these drugs can also become part of a victim's life support system, allowing him to self-medicate his way through the re-enactment of his original experiences of abuse and assault. Gender is now viewed in a far more fluid way than in Freud's day. While for some men the abdication of their core gender identity is not necessarily traumatogenic, for others it is part of a manic defence against the pain of being abused. The increasing sexualisation of the male body (in a way that tragically replays the objectification of women over the decades) provides more space for the victim to identify with his aggressor through starvation, overfeeding or compulsive and ultimately life-threatening drug-assisted exercise.

What has also changed is our understanding of dissociation and dissociative identity disorder, with the work of Sinason (see, for example, 1994, 2002) coming to inform a more relational approach to working with this most disabling response to early sexual attack. We also now have a deeper understanding of the impact of sexual trauma upon those on whom the male survivor depends for love, support and sustenance. I hope that this book alerts the clinical world to the need to pay attention to the needs of the primary patient's support network, as well as our own needs as practitioners. Sexual abuse has a toxicity that affects all those who come into contact with it. Unless we as psychotherapists are mindful of the potentially annihilatory impact of our work, we remain terribly vulnerable to burnout, breakdown or enactment.

Despite the many cultural and social changes that this book outlines, the heart of our work with patients remains broadly what it was in Freud's day. The key to our work is still relational, with the transference remaining an invaluable map to the internal traumatogenic landscape. The inclusion of this title in the Forensic Psychotherapy Monograph Series, however, indicates an important evolution in how we consider the experiences of the men with whom we work, both as survivors and as patients. We are no longer, or should no longer be, split in our responses to victims of sexual abuse. The fact that this book views them through the lens of forensic psychotherapy should not imply a view of victims as abusers in waiting. We must, however, be open to the notion that all survivors require of their therapist a forensic understanding. By this I mean forensic in its purest sense: a non-split view of the survivor through which we are able to see those aspects of him that act out as well as act in. Through this process we are in less danger of losing sight of the perpetrator within the victim or, indeed, the victim within the perpetrator.

CHAPTER ONE

The invisible men: a brief history of male survival

"I was invisible," says "Barry", his voice little more than a whisper. "No one saw me when I was growing up. There were so many of us I think my mam forgot about me a lot of the time. Apart from him. *He* saw me, all right."

Barry is referring to his parish priest in Ireland, the man whose sexual torture of him began at such an early age that Barry cannot recall a time in his life when he was not being abused. He looks barely visible, and seems more like a ghost than a man. His skin is pale, his body skinny and malnourished. I am used to working with male survivors of sexual abuse whose trauma remains hidden behind a veneer of apparent health, robustness and vigour, men whose outward demeanour offers no clues as to the horrors they have suffered. Barry is not like these other survivors, has no facade with which to cover his enduring pain. His defences are paper-thin and I marvel at how he is able to survive in this world. He is in his early thirties but looks much older, his skin dried and thinned by decades of cigarettes and alcohol. He has not worked for many years, and is currently scraping an existence on sickness benefit. He lives in a shared house, and spends most of his days in his room, his mind tormented by memories of the abuse that dominated his childhood. He is the personification of the word "victim". To call him a survivor would be to miss something completely evident about the way in which sexual abuse has drained all life from him.

My job is to assess Barry as part of his compensation claim against the Catholic Church and the Irish government, the two institutions most culpable for the crimes committed against him. He is one of many victims of this one priest who, when abuse was suspected or disclosed, was moved from one parish to the next, his abuses never defined as crimes and the actions of his employers enabling him to exploit another group of boys in another village or town. The work of getting from Barry a cogent narrative of his childhood abuse is easy. It is a story he has rehearsed in his head for many years and one that is all too credible. The most difficult task facing me now is deciding how to end our session. After two hours of outpouring the most unsettling and disturbing details of his abuse, I wonder if Barry is feeling as sick as I am. How, I wonder, will he be able to end this session and resume the barren, despairing, and empty life he has described? I tell him that I think he needs therapy. I remind him that he is entitled to free therapy, therapy that the Irish government will pay for. He smiles, sadly, and says he has tried it before. "But I had to stop. There was only enough money for two years. Two years! I was only getting started, and then I had to stop; I had to go back to my life. It'd take me a lifetime to say it all."

Eventually Barry was able to start low-cost therapy with a colleague of mine, someone used to working with men whose experiences of childhood abuse and, in some cases, adult rape, had imprinted upon them a translucence, an aura of invisibility. At first the work appeared to be going well, but I was unsurprised to learn that after a year Barry had stopped coming, the strain of revisiting his years of abuse becoming simply too much for him to bear. His therapist worked hard to keep Barry in treatment, trying to contain him through times of crisis when his alcohol use escalated and his capacity to simply get to the consulting room ebbed away. He vanished back into the state of invisibility he had described to me, a state that had left him vulnerable to abuse as a child and enabled him to slip through the cracks as an adult. Despite the prospect of the kind of long-term therapy he so clearly needed, the reality of his story and his self becoming visible were, perhaps, too much for him to bear. The safety of invisibility seemed to provide Barry with the refuge he yearned for, a refuge in which his suffering would continue, unheard and unseen.

A crime without a history

The invisibility of sexual trauma comes in many different forms. Some survivors, like Barry, occupy a fragile, wraithlike place in the world, their sense of self emaciated by neglect and further atrophied by abuse. Their trauma is etched onto their being to the point where we have to make them invisible—the agony with which they live is too much for us to see. There are other survivors who have managed to assume a pretence of pseudo-normality, whose histories of abuse are buried beneath layers of competency, internal damage hidden behind masks of high-functioning success. This too makes them invisible. We look at them and see nothing of the traumata that underpin their manic, inauthentic facade. This is possible partly because we do not wish to see. Visibility is not just dependent on what is seen, it relies on our capacity to look.

During the writing of this book, funding for London's only clinic specialising in working with male victims of sexual assault was cut. While this was a deep, life-changing shock to its clients and workers, the possible extinction of this well-established and highly regarded service did not trouble the headlines. There were no visible signs of protest, no marches, and no hunger strikes—just one online petition. What, I wondered, would have happened if there was only one clinic in London for female victims of sexual assault and it was threatened with sudden closure? I would hope and expect there to be mass protests, voices galvanised against such an appalling injustice, and appeals at the highest levels of government for sanity to prevail. How, then, is it possible for the killing-off of a service for men to be greeted with apathy, indifference, and near silence? How and why are boys and men who have been sexually abused rendered invisible?

There is something deeply problematic in how we consider the sexual abuse of boys and men. Scarce (2001) describes the rape and sexual assault of men as "a crime without a history", and it remains a phenomenon shrouded in the secrecy, shame, and fear that once characterised all forms of sexual abuse. The later part of the twentieth century saw the scales fall from our eyes in relation to sexual abuse, with the appalling experiences of children across the centuries finally being validated and given a place in both society and psychohistory (deMause, 1974).

And yet if we dare to speak of the rape and abuse of men, we speak in a whisper. While there still remains much work to be done in ensuring full legal justice for female victims of abuse, the work of feminist, social, and clinical action over the past forty years has ensured that a woman talking today about her abuse, as a girl or as a woman, is significantly more likely to be believed by those around her than twenty years ago.

Such a revolution has not happened for men. As will be demonstrated in this chapter and beyond, men are less likely than women to be believed if they summon up the courage to speak of their experiences of sexual abuse. This is an extraordinary finding, given what we already know about how hard women can struggle to have their experiences of abuse believed. There remains a collective societal blindness not only towards the experience of sexual abuse itself, but the resultant emotional needs of its male victims. In thinking about how we have fallen into such a dangerously split view of gender and abuse, I have considered some of the wider areas of denial enacted in such areas as the media and the criminal justice system, but have chosen to focus predominantly on the psychotherapy world. It is here where I hope this book may effect most change, loosening the grip of overly gendered attitudes towards sexual trauma, and allowing us as individual clinicians and representatives of training institutions to think more insightfully about the ways in which we invite male survivors into our consulting rooms.

Language

A few words first about terminology. "Sexual abuse" is a term that fails to capture the range and barbarity of the acts it seeks to describe, let alone the depth of suffering inflicted upon its victims. Since most of the clinical work with male survivors I will describe throughout this book took place in the UK (with some of the work taking place in the Republic of Ireland), I have used as my starting point the description found in the UK Government's guidance for professionals—*Working Together To Safeguard Children*—in which sexual abuse is defined as:

> Forcing or enticing a child or young person to take part in sexual activities, not necessarily involving a high level of violence, whether or not the child is aware of what is happening. The activities may involve physical contact, including assault by penetration (for example, rape or oral sex) or non-penetrative acts such as

> masturbation, kissing, rubbing and touching outside of clothing. They may also include non-contact activities, such as involving children in looking at, or in the production of, sexual images, watching sexual activities, encouraging children to behave in sexually inappropriate ways, or grooming a child in preparation for abuse (including via the internet). (DCSF, 2010, p. 38)

As we will see, this definition just about scratches the surface of the kind of experiences visited upon some boys, and does not say anything about the range and impact of abuses experienced in adult life. It is, though, a starting point, and one that I will seek to build on through a mixture of theory and practice. Alongside a bringing together of various theoretical strands, I will try to convey a fuller narrative of what sexual abuse is, the kind of visceral attack on both mind and body that it represents, and the particularly gendered responses it can generate in male survivors. The most effective way to convey the impact of sexual abuse and how to work with its effects therapeutically is to write about cases. In order to protect the confidentiality of the men I have worked with, I have disguised thoroughly every detail pertaining to them, to the point where the vignettes I have used should be viewed more as fictionalised accounts in which actual biographical details have been blended and blurred to the point of non-recognition. I will mainly use the term "male survivors" to describe the men I work, or have worked, with. I will occasionally use the word "victim", and have found myself using it mainly to describe those men for whom embarking on a psychotherapeutic process feels like an insurmountable hurdle, those for whom sexual trauma has had a crippling and potentially fatal impact.

Hidden in plain sight

Little about sexual abuse is new and the sexual abuse of boys and men is a phenomenon with a long but little-documented history. The means of abuse may evolve over time as abusers learn to make perverse use of the internet, social media, and global networking of paedophilia, but the process remains basically unchanged. Jimmy Savile's use of celebrity as a visible cloak (or to use the title of Davies' 2014 study of Savile's perversion being "hidden in plain sight") with which to hide his abuse of children and vulnerable adults is not a purely modern phenomenon. In 1895 a Manchester newspaper uncovered the crimes of

Gilbert Kirlew, a well-known and highly respected bastion of decency (Pavlakis, 2014). His fame, much like Savile's, was based partly on his very public acts of social good. He was at the vanguard of the new social movement to take poor children from the gutters into secure homes. It was at one of these homes that he was found to have been systematically sexually abusing the homeless and neglected boys he was supposedly giving refuge to.

The psychohistorian Lloyd deMause describes the story of childhood as "a nightmare from which we have only recently begun to awaken. The farther back in history one goes, the lower the level of child care, and the more likely children are to be killed, abandoned, beaten, terrorised, and sexually abused" (1974, p. 1). He goes on to describe the boy in antiquity living "his earliest years in an atmosphere of sexual abuse. Growing up in Greece and Rome often included being used sexually by older men ... In Crete and Boeotia, pederastic marriages and honeymoons were common. Abuse was less frequent among aristocratic boys in Rome, but sexual use of children was everywhere evident in some form. Boy brothels flourished in every city, and one could even contract for the use of a rent-a-boy service in Athens. Even where homosexuality with free boys was discouraged by law, men kept slave boys to abuse, so that even free-born children saw their fathers sleeping with boys" (p. 43). Intercourse with castrated boys was regarded as providing higher levels of arousal for men, with infants being castrated at extraordinarily young ages to be used in brothels. DeMause goes on to trace the history of childhood sexual abuse until the twentieth century, revealing a highly disturbing acceptance of the sexual objectification of infants, children, and adolescents of both genders.

Legal definitions

The Sexual Offences Act 2003 (England and Wales) defines rape as the non-consensual penetration of the vagina, anus, or mouth with a penis. The separate offence of sexual assault by penetration, which carries the same maximum sentence, covers attacks involving other objects. This legislation differs from that of other countries (including Scotland, Sweden, and the USA) that avoid gender-specific pronouns. Scotland's Sexual Offences Act in 2010 gave, for the first time, a legal definition of male rape, recognising that men, as well as women, could be victims. Despite its gendered definition of rape, changes to the England and

Wales Criminal Justice Act enabled the jailing of a man for life in 1995, for the attempted rape of another man. Change is happening, but at a painfully slow pace.

How the law conceptualises abuse does not simply have legal implications, it affects social and cultural attitudes. One common example of this is the assumption that a sexual assault cannot be regarded as a crime if the victim has an erection during the attack. Male erectile response is involuntary. A penis can become erect due to stimulation, not necessarily through arousal. The failure to understand this can be profoundly distressing for the victim who struggles to process the contradictory messages transmitted physiologically and psychologically: the mind screaming "no" and the body seeming to scream "yes." This confusion can also be seen in what in the United States have been referred to as "made to penetrate" cases, where male rape victims are made to engage in the penetration of a woman or a man. In many of these cases the male victims are under the influence of drugs or alcohol, or being held in life-threatening positions, and struggle afterwards with the guilt of what their body has done, against their conscious will.

Prevalence of sexual abuse

According to a study published in *Clinical Psychology Review* (Pereda et al., 2009) that examined sixty-five studies from twenty-two countries, the global prevalence of child sexual abuse has been estimated at 19.7 per cent for females and 7.9 per cent for males. The highest prevalence rate of child sexual abuse geographically was found in Africa (34.4 per cent), primarily because of high rates in South Africa. Europe showed the lowest prevalence rate (9.2 per cent) and America and Asia had prevalence rates between 10.1 per cent and 23.9 per cent. In the past, other research has concluded that in North America, for example, approximately 15 to 25 per cent of women and 5 to 15 per cent of men were sexually abused when they were children (Finkelhor, 1994; Gorey & Leslie, 1997).

In their study of self-reported childhood physical and sexual abuse in a general North American population sample of men and women, Briere and Elliott (2003) uncovered an incidence of 14.2 per cent of male subjects reporting sexual abuse as compared to 32.3 per cent of female subjects. Physical abuse was reported by 22.2 per cent of men, as compared to 19.5 per cent of women. Of subjects who had experienced one type of abuse, 21 per cent also experienced the other type, and both types were associated with subsequent adult victimisation. The gender breakdown of abusers of female victims was generally in line with the sexual abuse literature (93 per cent had been abused by at least one male, and 9 per cent had been abused by at least one female), whereas the data on perpetrator gender for male victims represented a newer finding. Of males who had experienced abuse, 39 per cent reported having been sexually abused by at least one female, and 70 per cent described sexual abuse by at least one male. Finkelhor (1994) extrapolated from available retrospective report studies that approximately 20 per cent of prepubescent boys who had experienced sexual abuse had been abused by a female. Mendel (1995) found that 60 per cent of his clinical sample of males reported childhood sexual contact with an older female. In 2012/13 the police in England and Wales recorded 5,156 offences of rape of a female child under sixteen, as compared to 1,138 offences of rape of a male child under 16. They also recorded 4,171 offences of sexual assault on a female child under thirteen as compared to 1,267 offences of sexual assault on a male child under thirteen (Office for National Statistics, 2013).

Under-reporting issues

Most disclosures of childhood sexual abuse take place some time, often years, after the abuse has occurred (Allnock & Miller, 2013). Girls are more likely than boys to disclose sexual abuse (Hanson et al., 2003; Tang et al., 2008; Terry et al., 2010). Research figures estimate that in the UK 11 per cent of the male population have suffered sexual abuse as children (Cawson et al., 2000), while 3.4 per cent of the male population have experienced sexual violation in adult life (Finney & Britain, 2006). These figures are, of course, subject to under-reporting issues. Prevalence estimates of adult sexual assault of men vary widely due to methodological inconsistencies among research studies (Peterson et al., 2011). The generally lower proportion of male as opposed to female victims of sexual abuse may not be completely accurate. Fewer than one in ten male–male rapes are reported (Crome, 2006). Under-reporting may be particularly prevalent for men because of the fear they will be labelled as homosexual (if the abuser was a man) or weak (if the abuser was a woman). Male victims of sexual abuse are also less likely than female victims to seek psychotherapeutic help at some point in their lives, although they are more likely than non-abused men to seek therapy for issues that seem unrelated to abuse (Gartner, 1999). Sexual abuse of girls is more common than abuse of boys, but it also more universally condemned when it is discovered (Groth, 1979).

Given the global prevalence of male abuse, the international silence about it is striking. Sivakumaran (2005) sees this silence as a communication of social homophobia. Society considers any sexual contact between men to be indicative of homosexuality, regardless of any element of coercion. Given the continuing prevalence of homophobia in society, this translates into a "taint" on the part of the victim of male rape. Holmes et al. (1997) suggest a conflation of two broad factors that lead to an under-reporting of male abuse: male victims are relatively unlikely to disclose their experience of childhood abuse, and (as a coping strategy) they deny the impact of sexual abuse on their lives. Professionals fail to hypothesise that their male clients may have been abused, and do not create the conditions that would enable males to talk about their abuse.

In their study into why some male survivors seek professional help and some do not, Masho and Alvanzo (2010) concluded that only 17.6 per cent of the male survivors they studied had sought help. The factors that increased the likelihood that a survivor would seek help included the presence of a physical injury, perpetration by family or friend, history of rape before the age of eighteen, and threat at the time of incident. In their research into male survivors' experiences of disclosure, Sorsoli et al. (2008) identified key factors that inhibited men in sharing their experiences of abuse. Some were not necessarily specific to their gender, such as lack of cognitive awareness, intentional avoidance, emotional readiness, shame, and fears about negative repercussions. Other, more sociocultural factors, were more gendered, specifically, the lack of acceptance for men to experience or acknowledge victimisation.

In his analysis of 390 cases of child sexual abuse, Levesque (1994) found that boys were significantly more likely than girls to have experienced oral intercourse, anal intercourse, and non-contact abuse. Boys are more likely than girls to be abused outside the home, subject to extra-familial abuse, and to be abused in the vicinity of witnesses. Vulnerability to being sexually abused increases if the boy has an intellectual disability, is subject to other forms of abuse within the home, has run away from home, or is in a hospital or institutional setting (Crome, 2006). Although the majority of perpetrators of abuse are male (Terry et al., 2010), boys are more likely than girls to be abused by a female (Tardif et al., 2005). One area where a higher incidence of male abuse exists is within clerical abuse: the rape and sexual assault of children and adults by priests, nuns, and other representatives of the Church (Ponton & Goldstein, 2004). This shows a higher than normal proportion of male as opposed to female victims, with Terry reporting that in his 2008 study 81 per cent of those sexually abused were boys.

Cases referred to the criminal justice system

Edelson (2013) examined two pilot studies investigating gender differences in whether cases of child sexual abuse were referred to the criminal justice system and, if they existed, what might account for gender differences in decisions to accept cases and file charges. The results of the first study indicated that cases involving male victims were *significantly* less likely to be accepted for prosecution than cases involving female victims. The reasons for this are extremely revealing:

1. Males were more likely to have been exposed to pornography or sexual activity than were females. Edelson suggests this exposure might make it more difficult to determine whether the presence of sexual knowledge (and concerning behaviour) was due to sexual abuse or to exposure to pornography.
2. Males were less likely than females to tell someone about the abuse, eliminating a potential witness who is able to testify about an individual's reporting of an event.
3. Males' initial disclosures were more likely than females' disclosures to occur in response to questions about the possibility of abuse (perhaps following the witnessing of concerning behaviour). This could lead to jurors suspecting that males' disclosures were suggested or coached.

Edelson concludes that it is not the quality of the disclosures of abuse that account for this gendered difference. Despite the *perception* that girls' disclosures are more credible than boys', research does not support the notion that females *actually* have more credible disclosures than males. Edelson and Joa (2010) found that cases involving male survivors were less likely to be accepted for prosecution and, once accepted, had fewer criminal counts charged and resulted in shorter sentences for defendants who pled or were found guilty. Wood et al. (1996) examined variables that related to the credibility of disclosures of sexual abuse made by children interviewed at a multidisciplinary assessment centre. They found that the disclosures of girls were perceived to be more credible than the disclosures of boys. Edelson (2013) noted that the differences found by Wood et al. were with regard to the *perception* of the credibility of the children's disclosures, not whether there were actual gender differences in the children's disclosures.

Stemple (2008) concludes that the international human rights framework is inadequate for addressing the problem of the sexual abuse of men and boys. She cites over 100 uses of the term "violence against women"—defined to include sexual violence—in United Nations (UN) resolutions, treaties, general comments, and consensus documents, but found no human rights instruments that explicitly addressed sexual violence against men. Sexual abuse has been infantilised, feminised, and homosexualised, and is difficult for any society to talk about without shame, confusion, and fear. These responses are softened when we can place male victims out of view and comfort ourselves with the notion that abuse only happens to innocent children, preferably girls. We are disturbed by the idea of a man as a victim, and further disturbed by having to think about any sexuality other than heterosexuality.

Media representation

There is something about the abuse of male victims that is deeply unsettling, as it touches on the complexities in conflating masculinity and victimhood, and challenges our deeply embedded notions of men as the aggressive victimisers and women as the passive victims. We lack a language with which to conceptualise this whole area of experience, as seen in the often infantile ways in which the abuse of boys is characterised by the British media. There is a vivid contrast between the reporting of cases of boys being abused by their female teachers and girls being abused, with the long term-emotional and behavioural impact of sexual violation tending to be correctly identified in the case of a girl being abused, and virtually ignored in the case of a boy. Newspaper headlines adopt a prurient, comical, and almost admiring tone. The boy is seen as having lived out an adolescent dream rather than being the victim of a crime, with stills from the 1967 film *The Graduate* being the images of choice with which to sanitise the abuse of any residue of exploitation, crime, or psychological damage. We are invited to envy rather than pity the victim.

Corrective rape

Male abuse is something that is affected by societal influences, and evolves and mutates according to the cultural factors surrounding it. "Corrective rape", for example, was first recorded in 2003 by the photographer Zanele Muholi and activist Kekeletso Khena in their campaign "The Rose Has Thorns", which documented the rape of lesbians in South Africa. The perpetrators' motives were ascribed to a misguided fantasy that by penetrating a lesbian her sexual orientation would somehow be transformed (and, in the distorted mindset of the perpetrator, "cured"). This barbaric practice has since expanded to target the transgender community, widening its catchment of victims to incorporate those born as men, as well as those choosing to live as men (Nath, 2011). An earlier report by the University of South Africa Centre for Applied Psychology (2003 study conducted by Out LGBT Well-Being and University of South Africa Centre for Applied Psychology; see Nel & Judge, 2008) found that the percentage of black gay men who said they had experienced corrective rape matched that of black lesbians who participated in the study. Here we can see a new variant of male abuse evolving and growing, not just against the backdrop of a traumatised and changing society, but because of it.

There is a link between how a society functions and the forms of abuse that flourish within it. There are also societal imperatives that help explain the invisibility of male survivors. In his study of male rape perpetrated against black slaves from the seventeenth to the nineteenth century, Foster (2011) described the rape of enslaved boys and men as being hidden in plain sight within the historical record, and further stated that no enslaved man would have been safe from sexual abuse. There are also inevitable links and connections between society, culture, place, and location. In her essay on "Notes on writing a novel", Elizabeth Bowen states: "Nothing can happen nowhere. The locale of the happening always colours the happening and often, to a degree, shapes it" (1975, p. 179). In his psychoanalytic study of maleness and masculinity, Blechner posits an imaginary initial consultation in which a patient describes aspects of his childhood:

> You discover that from age seven to twelve, he and many other boys were taken away from their families to a compound that was exclusively inhabited by men. It was a place where he was pushed to work, and, during leisure time, he sucked the penises of the older males in the compound. They told him that it was good for him, that ingesting other men's semen would make him manly, so that the more penises he sucked, the manlier he would become … The scenario I have just described is the norm for adolescent boys in a tribe in New Guinea that has been studied by Gilbert Herdt (1981) and which he calls the Sambians. (1998, p. 606)

Gartner argues that the context in which abuse has taken place is key to understanding whether it is traumatic or not: "For a Sambian boy, these experiences, which would be severely traumatic in American society, are therefore unlikely to be traumatic. If anything, they would probably be thought of with pride as his entrance to manhood" (1999, p. 135).

Rape in prisons

In looking at the uniquely closed society of prison life, we can see a hot-housing of male abuse. According to the organisation Human Rights Watch, twenty-two per cent of male prisoners experience sexual abuse while in US prisons (Mariner, 2001). Male prison rape has been described as "the most tolerated act of terrorism in the United States" (Robertson, 2002, p. 438). Male victims of abuse in prison have been found to be typically non-violent first-time offenders, with a study from one US prison showing that male homosexual prisoners were four times as likely as male heterosexual prisoners to become victims of rape and sexual assault (Wooden & Parker, 1982). No equivalent figures exist for the British prison system. A report by the Howard League for Penal Reform (Shaw, 2010) stated that the prison service had failed to investigate 1,443 recorded incidents of violent and sexual assaults in prisons. Out of 1,481 allegations of serious assaults in British prisons in 2008, the prison service only investigated 124, and out of 119 allegations of sexual assault in prison in the same year, only 33 investigations were conducted. The need to disavow, to look away from phenomena that are too painful and, perhaps, too confusing, to process, provides a false and faulty defence against reality.

Rape in warzones

Rape in war has traditionally been considered as a male on female phenomenon. Susan Brownmiller stated in her pioneering work *Against Our Will* that rape accompanied territorial advance as one of the spoils of war, and that "Men who rape are ordinary Joes, made unordinary by entry into the most exclusive male-only club in the world" (1975, p. 139). This perspective ignores a different narrative of male on male rape in war that is threaded throughout the history of conflict (Stemple, 2008) and first documented by the Roman historian Tacitus, who recorded how during the Revolt of the Batavi Roman military officers often used the young boys of defeated peoples for homosexual intercourse (Phang, 2001). Murals from the time of the Ancient Persians show the victors of battle parading with plates stacked high with their enemies' penises (DelZotto & Jones, 2002).

Most recent wars have featured the use of male rape as a weapon of war or a symbol of victory. The Yugoslavian Civil War was the first conflict for which an international body investigated the rape of men during the war. The team reported that men were castrated and otherwise sexually mutilated, forced to rape other men, and forced to perform fellatio and other sex acts on guards and one another (Bassiouni & McCormick, 1996). One study of 6,000 concentration camp inmates in Sarajevo found that eighty per cent of males reported that they had been raped while in detention (McGinn et al., 2004). According to a survey published in the *Journal of the American Medical Association* (Johnson et al., 2010) twenty-two per cent of men from the eastern part of the Democratic Republic of the Congo reported that they had been subject to conflict-related sexual violence. Stemple (2008) noted that sexual torture and rape were experienced by seventy-six per cent of male political prisoners in El Salvador during the Salvadoran Civil War.

Male captives were forced into sexual slavery during the conflicts in Liberia in the 1990s and early 2000s (Johnson et al., 2008); and the records of Sri Lankan men who had been referred to the Medical Foundation for the Care of Victims of Torture in 1997 and 1998, found that some men had been forced to masturbate their captors (Peel et al., 2000). This phenomenon of enforced masturbation was also documented in the rather better-known cases of abuse in Iraq, where men were found to have been tortured, sexually humiliated, and raped by both male and female American military staff in the Abu Ghraib detention facility

(Jones & Fay, 2004). An important component of the abuse of these men was the photographing of the various acts of sexual humiliation, described by Danner as a "shame multiplier" (2004, p. 72). The nebulous, fragile identities of these victims is captured in the official report's description of them as "ghost detainees" (p. 22), a term used to describe those combatants held in detention centres whose identity had been kept hidden. One of the most shocking forms of wartime abuse is what has been called "enforced rape" or "forced incest", in which men are forced to rape other victims, including family members or the dead (Sivakumaran, 2007, p. 263). Alongside this is the concept of "rape plus" (p. 264): a phenomenon documented during the conflict in Kosovo, in which the "plus" is the transmission of HIV/AIDS to the victim.

Hierarchy of sexual victimhood

Over thirty years ago the anthropologist Gayle Rubin (1984) theorised a hierarchical system of sexual value in which those practising "good" and "normal" sex were placed at the top of the social hierarchy, while those practising "bad" and "abnormal" sex were at the bottom. This notion has been subsumed into a wider discourse that tends to place victims of sexual abuse somewhere in a sexual victim hierarchy. At the top is the heterosexual, preferably virgin, white woman, raped by a stranger while sober, struggling throughout to resist. Bell et al. (1994) highlight the lower status of women who know their rapist (so called "date rape" or "acquaintance rape"), occupying a place on the hierarchy just above women judged to be promiscuous (meaning women who have had sex recently or with more than one partner within a short space of time). At the bottom of the ladder are sex workers, seen by many as being somehow to blame for the actions of the men who rape them.

We tend to struggle to know where to place men within this hierarchy of sexual victimhood. Those abused as boys are placed higher than those abused as men, with the identification of boys as more innocent victims carrying an implicit assumption that adult men carry some level of responsibility for the abuses perpetrated against them. The location in which the abuse occurs also seems to matter. Being raped in a park places a man higher on the hierarchy than if he had been raped in prison. Again, presumed innocence affects the level of compassion we extend to male victims. It is hard to think of a man as innocent if he has previously been branded as a perpetrator of crime, even a non-sexual one. Sexuality matters too. As gay men tend to tend to be placed at the bottom of a general gender hierarchy among men (Whitehead & Barrett, 2002), it is unsurprising that this is echoed in the placing of gay male victims at the bottom of the hierarchy of victimhood. Distorted and harmful stereotypes of male homosexuality—that gay men have abnormally high sex drives, that they are predatory, and that they are promiscuous—conspire to promote a view of gay victims of abuse as being complicit in their attack. Research into the attribution of blame amongst the British public found that respondents placed more blame on homosexual victims than heterosexual ones (Mitchell et al., 1999), as if gay victims have a conscious or unconscious desire to be raped. This echoes the positioning of women in the hierarchy according to perceived notions of promiscuity and desire.

Impact of sexual abuse

Gil's (2014) study compared fifty-eight males who had been sexually abused by males with thirty-nine males who had been sexually abused by females, in the domains of personality traits, trauma-related features, trauma-related psychopathologies, and fear of intimacy. The findings of the study revealed that male perpetrators were more aggressive and intensive in their abuse than female perpetrators, presumably generating greater psychopathology in their victims, including higher levels of neuroticism, post-traumatic stress disorder (PTSD) and dissociative symptoms, fear of exposure, fear of attack, and fear of one's own destructiveness. Male victims of female perpetrators exhibited diverse types of psychopathology, similar to those of their female abusers—higher levels of extraversion, agreeableness, fear of merger, and fear of abandonment. The findings of the study suggest that the perpetrator's gender is a differentiating factor in the profile of abuse among male survivors, and their reactions to it. Sexual abuse perpetrated by women can be difficult to detect, as it occurs within a seemingly intact relationship with no visible evidence of the child's resistance or distress. Indeed, intimacy between a mother and child is likely to be perceived positively and will rarely evoke suspicion, especially if the victims use latent coping strategies. We struggle to decode abuse within what should be the most secure domain, the mother/child dyad.

Research suggests that male survivors of child sexual abuse are more susceptible to internalising effects, while women are more likely to experience externalising effects (Romano & De Luca, 2001; Dorahy & Clearwater, 2012). This contrasts with findings from research in other areas indicating that men are more likely to externalise their problems. The difference may be related to gender norms that make it difficult for men to discuss sexual abuse, and possibly even to a cultural bias that sees women's, but not men's, promiscuity as an "externalising" problem (Cashmore & Shackel, 2013). In their study of the overrepresentation of male survivors in mental health and other clinical populations, O'Leary and Gould (2010) found that the coping strategies used by men fell into one of two broad clusters: those who had tended to suppress and deny their abuse, and those who had "reframed" the abuse with the help of consistent, supportive relationships with others. Unsurprisingly, the first group experienced far poorer mental health outcomes than the second. The type and quality of trauma associated with rape may be different from other forms of trauma because of the high incidence of self-blame, concurrent depression, and the increased risk of suicide (Kimerling et al., 2002).

Childhood trauma has been linked to a variety of changes in brain structure and function (Anda et al., 2006). Survivors of abuse have significantly higher rates of psychiatric treatment than the general population, with higher specific rates for childhood mental disorders, personality disorders, anxiety disorders, and major affective disorders. Childhood mental disorders, in particular, are higher for men than for women, although generally male survivors are significantly more likely than female survivors to have had contact with mental health services (Spataro et al., 2004). This runs counter to the assumption often made that women are more likely than men to disclose their experiences of abuse and then seek treatment of some kind (Watkins & Bentovim, 1992).

The relatively new wave of interest in epigenetics is developing ways of examining the impact of abuse. Genome research (Mehta et al., 2013) shows that PTSD patients who were abused as children have different patterns of DNA methylation and gene expression compared to those who were not. Despite sharing a few common biological pathways, ninety-eight per cent of the changes in gene expression patterns in PTSD patients with childhood abuse did not overlap with those found in PTSD patients without childhood abuse. Furthermore, the researchers found that epigenetic marks associated with gene expression changes were up to twelve-fold higher in PTSD patients with a history of childhood abuse. This suggests that although all patients with PTSD may show similar symptoms, abused children who subsequently develop PTSD may experience a systematically and biologically different form of the disorder compared to those without childhood abuse.

This echoes Read et al.'s (2009) challenge to the "medical model" view of trauma, largely supported by the pharmaceutical industry, with its reductionist focus on biological phenomena and minimal consideration of the social context within which genes and brains inevitably operate. They point to this ideology having been particularly powerful in the field of psychosis, and call for an epigenetic perspective to be adopted that could help us understand more about the impact of severe childhood trauma on the development of psychotic episodes and states.

Sexual abuse results in physiological as well as psychological trauma. Leserman (2005) demonstrated that abuse appears to be related to greater likelihood of headache, gastrointestinal, and panic-related symptoms, with abuse involving penetration and multiple incidents appearing to be the most harmful. For many male victims, the aftermath of the abuse can be as traumatising as the abuse itself. The marginalisation of male victims, on both a societal and an individual level, is captured movingly in this excerpt from a report in the Guardian:

> [B]oth perpetrator and victim enter a conspiracy of silence and [this is] why male survivors often find, once their story is discovered, that they lose the support and comfort of those around them. In the patriarchal societies found in many developing countries, gender roles are strictly defined … Often … wives who discover their husbands have been raped decide to leave them. They ask me: "So now how am I going to live with him? As what? Is this still a husband? Is it a wife?" They ask, "If he can be raped, who is protecting me?" (Storr, 2011)

Abuse and masculinity

Invisibility is generally defined as either something that is impossible to see or something that is hidden. Just as Harrington stated that, "The poor are politically invisible" (1962, p. 6), I believe that a combination of political, social, and clinical factors have conspired to airbrush the male survivor from our consciousness. The extent to which girls and women are subject to sexual abuse has been made visible by a largely feminist political movement able to chart the connections between societal powerlessness and sexual vulnerability. This has traditionally been a difficult link to make with men, given the myriad ways in which they are valorised as powerful, potent masters of their domain. Making male survivors visible involves letting go of deeply embedded societal and psychological expectations concerning men and masculinity.

Mosse (1998) dates the birth of modern masculinity as occurring between the second half of the eighteenth century and the beginning of the nineteenth, heralding an era in which the male body became the chief signifier of manliness, symbolising power and control. This ideal of masculinity soon became militarised, with the First World War seeing a resurgence in the ideal of masculinity. Aggression became idealised and vulnerability denigrated. Marginalised groups were systematically excluded from stereotypical ideals, becoming exemplars of ugliness and effeminacy. Popular culture and the birth of the "new man" have challenged this narrative of masculinity to some extent, but we continue to equate maleness with power, denigrating vulnerability and powerlessness as signifiers of something effeminate or anti-male. We can, just about, tolerate the thought of a woman as a victim of sexual abuse, because it confirms our stereotypical conflation of femininity and weakness. To consider a man as a victim of sexual aggression threatens to unravel our tightly knit assumptions as to the unconscious power role of the father, the function of phallic masculinity, and the gendered character of the superego. For us to irradiate the presence of the male survivor requires a loosening of the grip of some of our assumptions about the relationship between vulnerability, trauma, and gender. This is a process that requires of us a capacity to look unflinchingly at the experiences of men who have experienced sexual violation.

Stories written in invisible ink

Barry is one of many men whose stories have been written in invisible ink. His years of abuse and trauma have caused him to display a fatal level of ambivalence. His pleas for help are diluted by his resistance to being helped, and his tendency to flee from the demands of a therapeutic relationship make his story a doubly tragic one. His inability to sustain therapy for as long as he needs to means that, not only does he fail to benefit from a reparative and potentially healing experience, we as a profession fail to learn how best to help him. Barry's story is not unique. There are untold men whose sense of self is so porous and fragile that we have a responsibility to construct new ways of engaging with them. It is my hypothesis that shame inhibited Barry from allowing himself to be helped. He was unable to let go of the belief that his abuse was deserved and, as such, could never believe that he deserved to be helped. Psychotherapy is an intensive process that requires a readiness on the part of the patient to bear to look afresh at the causes of their pain—in itself, a painful process. Throughout this book I wish to consider what is the specific impact of sexual abuse upon boys and men and, in doing so, wish also to question how best we can adapt our practice to accommodate particularly gendered responses to abuse. This involves examining whether there are specifically male responses to sexual abuse that require specifically gendered therapeutic responses. Unless this question can be answered in some way, the likelihood is that men like Barry, and the other men described in the following chapters, will continue to be hidden from view.

CHAPTER TWO

Toxic masculinity: the impact of sexual aggression upon the male psyche

"Gary" slouches into the consulting room, falling into the chair and staring at "Kate", his therapist, with utter contempt. He is dressed in jeans, a denim jacket, and a tight white t-shirt. He takes off his jacket and throws it across the couch, revealing arms crowded with tattoos. Small patches of skin nestle between large, garish tattoos proclaiming "Hate", "Murder", and "Die". His hair is shaved close to his skull, and his earlobes are weighed down by crosses and skulls that glint against the overhead light. Kate swallows hard, aware of feelings of fear and anxiety tightening inside her. She has read his file before, is aware of his history of sexual abuse as well as the litany of burglaries and violent assaults he has perpetrated over the years. He has been referred to her to assess whether he can make use of once-weekly psychotherapy. The referral has been driven by his probation officer who is aware of Kate's expertise in working with sexual abuse and her track record in engaging with men who others have failed to reach. She introduces herself and, as she does so, Gary takes out a cigarette and goes to light it.

"Sorry," she says, "you can't smoke in here." He laughs, lights the cigarette and takes a few long drags on it before squeezing it to death.

"Just fancied a quick one," he says with a grin. She takes this as a cue to talk about the ground rules of the session, the boundaries he will need to observe for them to work safely together, and he gazes out the window, seemingly uninterested in anything she has to tell him. She seeks to reassure him that this can be a safe space, and that she is someone who can bear to hear whatever he has to tell her. He laughs again, and says his probation officer told him it would be good to talk about all the things that happened to him in his childhood. "I know all that crap—it's good to talk. You've probably read about it all anyway; no point in telling you." Kate acknowledges that, yes, she has read about some of the terrible events from his childhood, but what she doesn't know is what he made of them, how they have affected him.

"Just normal," he says, after a brief silence. "That's just life. Shit happens. Bastard touched me up, so I gave him what for. That's what happened." Kate reflects back to him that perhaps it was terrible that it happened to him, and that he might still struggle with remembering it. Gary seems to ponder on this for a few moments, and then explains to Kate that she seems to be under the impression that he is some kind of victim of abuse. "But I'm not. He was a dirty bastard; I know that. But I was a dirty bastard too. Still am. He touched me up because he knew I'd be up for it. And then soon enough I was doing more: sucking him off, getting him to fuck me. I was in charge. He thought he'd make me feel like nothing—he didn't have a clue."

Gary had been sexually abused by a friend of his mother. The abuse had continued for some years, starting when Gary was three and ending only when he entered puberty. In the session Gary goes on to talk about the abuse in great detail, recounting the physical features of it with what seems to Kate to be an aggressive enjoyment, as if recalling the details of a particularly brutal but strangely compelling film. Unlike other patients who recount their abuse with trepidation, feeling, and deep hurt, Gary seems to be treating it as a story with which he can cause Kate harm, using each increasingly vivid and disgusting memory as a weapon with which to batter her.

Partly as a way of shutting down this attack upon her, Kate encourages Gary to tell her about his family, most particularly his mother. "Bit of a cow," Gary declares. "But I knew how to deal with her. Didn't let her get away with anything. She knew who was boss." This unleashes a tirade of verbal abuse from Gary, and again he seems strangely exhilarated, caught up in a rising tide of perverse excitement. As Gary rails against the failings of his mother Kate finds herself feeling pummelled by him, while also feeling deeply confused. His narrative is at odds with all that Kate has read in Gary's file about a harsh, emotionally abusive mother who subjected him to a childhood of terror and servitude, and who was eventually forced to admit her inability to mother him before his being taken into care.

Later in the session Kate returns to Gary's description of abuse, and wonders aloud whether he might be missing something from his narrative. Something like fear, or hurt. Most little boys feel scared when bad things happen to them or around them. What did he do with his fear? There is a long silence, a silence that seems absolutely riven with anxiety and an unbearable tension. Suddenly Gary leaps up and slams his fist down on the table by Kate's chair. "You deaf or something?" he bellows. "Thought I'd told you. *He's* the one who was frightened, not me. *Him*!" Kate chooses, wisely, to back off from this point, and as the session comes to a close Gary says he probably won't be returning for next week's meeting, as he can see no point in wasting his time with her. "Unless," he adds, staring at her breasts, "you wanna flash your tits a bit more, make it worth my while." He laughs again, and leaves the room.

* * *

Boys will be boys: what this tends to mean in contemporary society is that boys will be strong and tough, growing up to be men who are independent, assertive, and sexually potent. Anything less than this implies a failure of masculinity (Lillywhite & Skidmore, 2006). Gary's engagement with Kate raises the question of whether there is a specifically gendered response to sexual trauma: do men experience sexual violation in different ways from women? His aggression and sadistic attack upon his therapist would seem, on the surface, to conform to a markedly hyper-masculine orientation. In her study of the "feminisation of victimisation", Sepler states that:

> the subjective experience of a male victim is decidedly different from that of a female victim. In many cases, the duration and nature of sexual encounters between a male child and his perpetrator bear the external trappings of consensual contact. Like a veil, the notion of consent conceals the underlying coercion and manipulation experienced by the victim. Loss of control, or being

> overpowered, a familiar theme of girls and women who have been sexually abused, may be emotionally inaccessible or inexplicable to male victims. The dynamic of vulnerability lies outside the emotional vocabulary of many "normal" males. (1990, p. 77)

Psychosocial constructs

Sepler locates this phenomenon within a psychosocial construct in which the socialisation of boys privileges them as masters of their domain, their self, and their environment. More fundamentally, they tend to be socialised to think of themselves as masters of others. Gary is seen through this vignette to be enacting a dynamic that is all too painfully familiar to many survivors of abuse. He finds himself in a position of impotence: the powerless patient sitting opposite the omnipotent therapist, the holder of power. His capacity to acknowledge openly his terror at having to grant dominance to another—particularly to a woman—has been atrophied not just by his experiences of sexual abuse, but by his object-relational history. He has to defend against his terror by attacking the one who most terrifies him. His squeeze of the cigarette is a frightening taste of the threat of murderous and sexualised rage that is threaded throughout his whole presentation. In this situation Kate is not just his therapist. In the transference she is, amongst others, his mother and his abuser. His denigration of women is a living metaphor not just for his hatred of his mother, but for those feelings of his own that feel too feminine: fear, weakness, fragility. Faced with this compound of vulnerability there is little available to him that can help him make sense of the terror he feels. He has to sublimate it into a powerful force that terrorises others, leaving him seemingly free of fear.

Janoff-Bulman's (1992) "shattered assumptions" theory touches on the impact of trauma upon those whose previous assumptions had centred on the world being a generous and virtuous place. She suggests that the disintegration of these views represents a far greater trauma than that of people whose assumptions were already that the world is unpredictable and dangerous. I suggest this is not a terribly compelling theory, positing as it does a hierarchy of trauma in which those with chaotic early life experiences are necessarily less affected by abuse than those with non-traumatic beginnings. As Wasco (2003) points out, many survivors of sexual abuse have already experienced other profound traumata. The later sexual trauma assault may not necessarily shatter their worldview because they have already experienced the world as chaotic and unjust. It may, as was the case for Gary, serve instead to horribly magnify their worldview. Sexual abuse in its myriad forms will always be a traumatic experience, and the effects of this trauma for an individual will be different in different contexts.

Pseudoconsensual postures

In recounting his experience of sexual abuse Gary is disavowing the reality of his age (he was three when the abuse began) and of his status as a victim. He was unable to consent, on any level, legal or emotional, to any kind of sexual activity. He was a child who needed protection and in its place found punishment of the most visceral, abusive kind. Yet he has to present himself as being on the same level, or above, as his abuser—speaking of himself as if he were an adult too, able to consent in a mutually desired sexual relationship. Gary is adopting what Sepler calls a *pseudoconsensual posture* (1990, p. 78), by which he is turning his experiences of victimhood, threat, and fear into more acceptable feelings of power and control. No doubt this valency predates his experiences of sexual abuse, and may have been laid down as the default position of his internal objects at a terribly young age. He is as much a victim of his mother's harsh, depriving maternal style as he is of her boyfriend's sexual attacks. This differs from Summit's (1983) concept of the accommodation of sexual abuse by female victims in its more intense notion of mastery and control. In cognitively reframing their experiences of abuse, men are more likely to seek to split off from their experiences of powerlessness, replacing them with displaced feelings of agency over the act of abuse. Sepler argues that men are unlikely to view themselves as victims in the feminine sense of the word. Rather, "many, if not most, young male victims will quickly make and then reinforce the psychological, physical or social adjustment that leads them to emulate consent or volition" (Sepler, 1990, p. 77).

Gary's ambivalence about returning for further sessions with Kate was a marker of how fearful he was of examining those more "feminine" feelings of fear and terror that Kate was inviting him to consider. As Kate recounted later in supervision, she was left with a devastating sense of terror after he left. She found herself hoping that he would not return for a follow-up session so she would not have to be in the presence and, more importantly, on the receiving end of such overwhelming anxiety. Gary was having to ignore the real dynamics of his abuse in favour of a bizarre fiction in which he, the child, held the power to exploit the adult man. This was his attempt to keep at bay unacceptable and disavowed feelings of helplessness and vulnerability. The primary motives powering most acts of sexual abuse are aggression, dominance, and anger. Sex is merely a weapon used to inflict violence and humiliation on a victim. Gary directed his sexual slur at Kate not because of any particular sexual interest he held about her; he was more interested in knowing she was someone who could be humiliated and belittled through threatened aggression. His biggest problem emerged when he was unable to disentangle the two: when his need to make the world feel the terror and fragility he could not bear to feel spilled over into concrete, physical attacks. He was a dangerous man, whose threat lied in the seeming impossibility of him being able to acknowledge the agony of being abused.

Attacks on masculinity

We can see here how Gary has experienced his sexual abuse primarily as an attack on his masculinity, backing up Gartner's (1999) view that the man fears that in being identified as a victim of sexual abuse he will lose his masculine identity. Goldner (1991) refutes the notion of a core masculinity, arguing that it is a cultural notion inculcated through socialisation. This touches on a feminist psychoanalytic view that in sexual situations men are taught to and expect to be *desiring subjects* who initiate and take control of sex (Dimen, 1991; Benjamin, 1996). The experience of sexual abuse subverts this in a profound way, with the male survivor taking the role traditionally ascribed to the woman, that of the *desired object*. This subversion of role is too much for many male survivors to bear, being experienced as a catastrophic attack upon the male sense of self.

In describing a key goal of therapy as being the "remasculinisation of sexually abused men" Gartner (1999, p. 88) is saying something inarguable about the need to attend to a particularly gendered wound felt by men who have been sexually abused: "At heart, the fear of being penetrated, like many fears related to masculine gender identity struggles, is a fear of forfeiting a self-definition as a man. This self-concept was achieved through *disidentifying* with qualities that signify being either female or homosexual" (pp. 76–77). Elise (2001) discusses the masculine sense of self being dependent on an impermeable psychic boundary into which no intrusions can be tolerated. The breaking into this boundary is not experienced solely as a penetration of the body but, more importantly, of the mind, leading to a shattering of the core identity, of which masculinity is an inextricable foundation. A core fear felt by many male survivors is that the experience of being sexually abused may somehow alter their sexual orientation, denying them the heterosexual role so validated by society in favour of the more stigmatised and disavowed homosexual position. Finkelhor (1994) found from his observation of boys growing up to be homosexual that they were disproportionately more vulnerable to sexual exploitation, and he concluded that childhood abuse was in some way the cause of their later sexual orientation. However, this has been refuted by those researchers who place the establishment of sexual orientation before the latency period, with most sexual abuse of boys occurring after this stage.

Theories of sexuality

Bieber et al. (1962) surveyed various theoretical schools of thought into homosexuality, and suggested that they fall into two major categories: those assuming adult homosexuality to be a psychopathological state and those assuming homosexuality not to be psychopathological, but simply an expression of a natural polymorphous sexuality. Freud's views on homosexuality have been variously read as either virulently homophobic or deeply tolerant. His non-pathologising view of homosexuality may be seen in his support for the decriminalisation of homosexual acts in Germany and Austria (Abelove, 1986) and his view that seeking to address society's antagonistic view of homosexuality was preferable to seeking to "cure" the homosexual patient (Wortis, 1954). His central theory of sexuality is that we are by nature bisexual, with homosexuality arising from insufficient repression of the original bisexual disposition. This indicates a negation of parity between homo- and heterosexuality, although his studies of homosexual figures such as Plato, Michelangelo, and da Vinci (Freud, 1905d, 1910c) helped give voice to a startlingly clear statement in a 1903 interview, quoted in *Die Zeit*, (and later quoted by Lewes, 1988, pp. 19–20):

> I am of the firm conviction that homosexuals must not be treated as sick people ... Wouldn't that oblige us to characterize as sick many

> great thinkers and scholars whom we admire precisely because of their mental health? Homosexual persons are not sick. They also do not belong in a court of law.

All psychotherapeutic work with male survivors involves an examination of homosexuality. The patient's relation to his own sexuality will be coloured by trauma. Those abused in childhood may fear, if they are gay, that their homosexuality is a consequence of sexual violation. If they are heterosexual they may struggle to accommodate within their self-conceptualisation the residue of arousal, or excitement that abuse can leave behind. If they have been assaulted or raped as an adult similar uncertainties may impinge upon their notion of their sexuality. Internalised homophobic thoughts and feelings can be activated for both homo- and heterosexual survivors through the experience of being abused by another man.

Trauma

The experience of being sexually abused is an all-encompassing psychological and physiological trauma that differs in small and significant ways from other non-sexual traumata. Trauma is a Greek word meaning a wound, lesion, or injury, and stems from the verb "to pierce" or "to penetrate". The Greek, Sanskrit, and Persian origin of the word *tere,* to which the word trauma is related, dates back to 1500 BC and refers to an "open hole" in the body, while also capturing the sense of "passing through or changing from a state without the hole to a state with the hole" (Wilson & Lindy, 2013, p. 35). Another etymological root is the verb *teiro,* which means to rub. From this stems the verb *titrosko,* meaning to pierce. This has multiple meanings in ancient Greek: to rub in, to rub away, or to rub off. So trauma may be "the mark left by either a wound (the result of an experience being *'rubbed in'*) or a process of cleansing; the result of an experience having *'rubbed* something *off'* or *'rubbed* it *away'*. Trauma can be the result of an injury or the result of a cleansing" (Papadopoulos, 2002, pp. 171–172). Wilson and Lindy describe trauma as "an unformed and incomplete wordless state of psychobiological processes … to describe the event externally and internally and to break it down into workable elements, the survivor will need to build a new language to express these words and phrases in narrative forms" (2013, p. 41). In her paper on the trauma of shell shock in the First World

War, Bourke (2014) highlights the unspoken stem of the word trauma: the piercing sting of perpetration. The word initially held the duality of injury, the ways in which the process of being pierced can also contain within it the fantasy, potential, or reality of piercing. Bourke contextualised this from the perspective of those soldiers on either side in the Great War whose symptoms of shell shock stemmed not only from being the recipients of injury, but also from being the bringers of, not just injury, but maiming and death.

The trauma of sexual abuse is never just the trauma of victimisation. One reason why so many survivors (of both genders) struggle so painfully with a pervading sense of shame is that, like the shell-shocked soldiers of the First World War, the experience of being wounded has become enmeshed with the experience of wounding. The abuser is unconsciously (and sometimes consciously) adept at transforming the victim's body into a weapon. The physiological responses to being sexually abused can include, to the horror of the victim, feelings of perverse excitement and arousal, alongside terror, rage, and numbness. This deeply confusing set of bodily responses is sometimes compounded by the abuser, who knows the power of telling his or her victim that he is to blame for the abuse, that he invited it, or that he cannot tell anyone else about it because they would know that he himself brought it about. Even without these perverse distortions on the part of the abuser, the victim is left shell-shocked by his own body's capacity for an apparent collusion with the act of abuse.

Impact of early family dysfunction

Working with Gary involved working with an internalised and perverse family system. Understanding and thus withstanding his sadistic attacks upon her and the therapeutic frame involved Kate having to attune to at least two traumata: the trauma of having been sexually abused and the trauma of early family dysfunction. Alexander (1992) considers family context to be a risk factor for the onset of sexual abuse and as a mediator of its long-term effects. She points specifically to the absence of a biological parent, maternal physical or emotional unavailability, marital conflict and violence, the child's poor relationship with the parents, and the presence of a stepfather. She further suggests that many of the long-term effects of sexual abuse are associated more with family characteristics than abuse-specific characteristics.

Kate's work with Gary was a long project involving the slow and gradual peeling away of layers of defensive aggression. He tended to oscillate between belligerence and vulnerability, requiring of Kate a capacity to modulate her therapeutic stance and adjust the levels of interpretative work he could withstand. Eventually it became more possible for Gary to lower his facade of anger and hostility, and allow Kate to glimpse the frightened child that hid beneath it. It involved as much delicate attention to be paid to his experiences of family trauma as to his history of sexual abuse. It was clear that the traumata were interwoven and in many ways fed off each other. Interestingly, Kate's greatest challenge lay in working out how and when to end her work with Gary. The fear that gripped her at the start of the work was replaced by powerful feelings of attachment and respect for the dignified way in which he confronted the spectres of his youth. Their final year of work together was one in which it became increasingly clear that Gary had formed a new narrative of his early life. Ending was unbearable for him, and he managed the process by absenting himself from the last few sessions, his sudden invisibility serving as a powerful reminder of the impact of being understood by another. In the end this was too much for him to say goodbye to.

Re-enactment of sexual aggression

Psychotherapy with male survivors is a form of forensic psychotherapy, examining as it does the internalised and externalised aftermath of sexual abuse. While not wishing to deny the reality of women survivors who externalise their experiences of trauma through murderous aggression (Welldon, 1988; Motz, 2001), it appears to be a phenomenon that men are more vulnerable to enacting. The intense feelings of powerlessness engendered by sexual abuse and rape present an existential challenge to the male, socialised as he is to conform to societal notions of strength, dominance, and potency. The particular sexual trauma of abuse touches on fears of homosexuality, producing an internal state of war between feelings of arousal, excitement, and revulsion. The need to defend against terrifying feelings of impotence is particularly intense for the male survivor, necessitating the erecting of defences that, in the case of Gary and others, are constructed from murderous rage and violent aggression. In working with such patients it can be difficult for the therapist to attune to the frightened, helpless child within. The trauma of sexual abuse becomes an encapsulated one, hidden beneath layers of cruelty, brutality, and hatred. We have to work hard to avoid an unhelpfully split view of our patients in which all we attend to are the hostile, dangerous defences, deflecting us from the primary task of locating the vulnerability that lies beneath. We must also attend to the failure of many patients to dare to think of themselves as victims, preferring the more powerful mantle of aggressor. The experience of sexual abuse with all its attendant feelings of vulnerability and powerlessness may be one that is encoded in the psyche, requiring of us a forensic vigilance alongside a patience, a knowledge that premature interpretations about the victim experience will serve only to magnify the patient's aggressive defences. We are dealing with men whose experiences of sexual trauma equate to a loss of the masculine self. This is a loss that requires validation and a slow, gradual process of therapeutic mourning before there can be an authentic sense of validation and healing.

CHAPTER THREE

Numbers: working with sexual compulsion

"Tony" grew up in the midst of perversion and madness. He was the only child of a mother who had been diagnosed with a violent personality disorder, and who had spent long periods of Tony's childhood in various psychiatric hospitals. His father was unknown to him, and those periods in which his mother was hospitalised saw him being cared for by his maternal grandmother. This continued until the age of ten, at which point Tony's grandmother died. His relationship with his grandmother was an intense and disturbing one, and it is clear now that she shared much psychiatric ill-health with her daughter. Tony could not remember a time when his grandmother did not subject him to intrusive sexual touch. Most of her abuse of him occurred at liminal times—as he was waking or drifting off into sleep—times that imbued her abuses with a dim, dream-like hue. When he was five years old and had to go to school, a split was created between the Tony who inhabited his grandmother's home, and the Tony who was forced to repress the nightmare of his home life and project an image of happy normality. There were times when, returned to the care of his mother, he tried to tell her something of the attacks his grandmother was making on his body. His mother appeared frightened whenever Tony tried to raise this, urging him to stop, telling him to, "Stop your silly talking. Nanny would never do anything naughty."

Adolescence and the onset of puberty were, unsurprisingly, times of deep confusion for Tony, tortured as he was by the memories of his grandmother's actions. He realised his primary sexual attraction was towards other males, but for a long time fought against this desire, fearing his grandmother's actions had perverted his sexual orientation. His sexuality was shrouded in secrecy, and it became difficult for Tony to think of sexual desire without feeling overwhelmed by a pervasive and debilitating sense of shame. He made some half-hearted attempts to engage in sexual relationships with girls his own age, but these abortive, desireless encounters merely added to his sense of sexual failure. He developed an interest in pornography, beginning with printed imagery and progressing to a world of internet porn that soon enveloped him and escalated quickly into a compulsion, a habit that provided him with a short-lived relief from his ongoing sense of frustration and self-hatred.

Tony struggled to develop any relationships with boys and men as he grew up. The more he was forced to realise that he lacked the skills to engage with men in any kind of pleasurable, reciprocal relationship, the heavier his dependence on pornography grew. In his early twenties he began to explore the world of anonymous sex. Using various websites and mobile phone apps he discovered a world in which he could click onto an online profile and within half an hour be engaging in frenzied and almost completely anonymous sex. The objects of this form of desire varied in age—the most important factor being their lack of interest in him as a human being. At any sign of curiosity about him, or desire to arrange to meet again, Tony would immediately disengage.

His decline was accelerated by his entry into the world of chemsex. Chemsex is a term used to describe sex that occurs under the influence of drugs, taken immediately preceding and/or during the sexual session. The drugs most commonly associated with chemsex are crystal methamphetamine, GHB/GBL, mephedrone, and, to a lesser extent, cocaine and ketamine. All except ketamine are stimulant drugs in that they typically increase heart rate and blood pressure, and trigger feelings of euphoria. Crystal methamphetamine, GHB/GBL, and mephedrone also have a common effect of facilitating feelings of sexual arousal. These drugs are widely known to facilitate pleasure or euphoria but are also associated with a range of harms. Particular concern has been raised regarding the role of crystal meth, GHB/GBL, and mephedrone in increasing risk behaviours that can lead to sexually transmitted diseases, including HIV (Bourne et al., 2014).

Tony soon found himself submerged in a world of anonymous, drug-fuelled sexual encounters. Sexual sessions lasted, at times, for days. The more he attended, the further he became detached from the pressures of his life. This world of chemical-fuelled desire appeared at first to provide a refuge from all that Tony could not bear to think about: his abuse, his feelings of shame about his sexuality, his fear of intimacy, and the pressures of his work. All those things that caused him such distress and anxiety while sober seemed to fall away from him the more he engaged in this new world with its promise of wild sex and no consequences.

It took Tony a long time to reveal to me his history of abuse and his sexual compulsions. Fairly early into our work he alluded to problems he had with getting to work on time. "It's getting harder to wake up—I tend to be a night owl," he said, explaining both his difficulties in getting to work on time and his growing lateness for his therapy sessions. Time was a perennial problem for Tony, causing a perpetual lateness and occasional absence from sessions, something he commented upon as taking place in every part of his life. "It's not as if I mean to be late for everything," he said, a slight curiosity colouring his flat, monotone voice. "It's just that sometimes I lose complete track of time. It doesn't have any meaning." Something about his description of himself as a night owl, a slight whisper of something disturbing and puzzling beneath his words, registered a note of curiosity and alarm in me. His attendance became sporadic, and his messages apologising for his unexplained absences stopped coming. He initially flicked away any attempts by me to explore this further, and it was some months before he began, slowly, gradually, and with an enormous amount of shame, to disclose how he tended to spend his hours as a night owl: his twin addictions to internet pornography, and to compulsive, drug-fuelled sex with strangers. My attempts to work with both pathologies stalled for some months until, in an intensely painful session, Tony began to form connections between his behaviour and his history of childhood abuse. During this outpouring of his narrative Tony displayed an almost complete lack of affect, his voice remaining curiously flat as he related the most distressing elements of his story. Nothing, no horrific detail of abuse or memory of humiliation at the hands of his grandmother, seemed to stir any life in his tone. I found myself overwhelmed by the bleakness of his story, noticing that all the feeling seemed to be being held by me rather than by him.

Tony was frightened of telling me the extent of his immersion into the world of chemsex. He feared that I would either misunderstand his reasons for falling into this world or would reject him because of my disgust at the nature of his sexual desires. It was a world that was, at times, difficult to comprehend, a world in which the most sexually intimate acts were enjoyed by the least intimate of strangers. Tony described days spent with men whose names he rarely knew but whose body parts became as familiar to him as his own. The mixture of drugs underpinning all sexual encounters lent a strange hue to Tony's memories, with the narrative of these "missing days" oscillating between a cinematic vibrancy and a hazy, dreamlike miasma. The fusion of bodies was described by Tony as akin to a blurring of definition, with him rarely knowing where his body ended and that of another man began. There was something of Freud's polymorphous perversity about these glimpses of undifferentiated need that left me feeling as if some numbing, bewildering drug had been implanted in me. I struggled to keep track of the multifarious ways in which sexual gratification was derived by Tony, his oral, anal, and phallic needs fused in a highly charged erotic drama that ebbed and flowed as the chemicals he had ingested whirled around his brain.

My attempts to project any relational meaning into these chemically enhanced orgies were rejected by Tony. I often mistook sexual intimacy for relational intimacy, my wires getting dangerously crossed as I sought to hope that some relationship might emerge from the synthesis of bodies that Tony had sculpted himself inside. "That's not the point," he reprimanded me in one session. "I'm not there to find a partner. I'm there to feel, to be alive. Relationships just don't come into it." This came as a surprise to me, as Tony had just five minutes before been recalling a deep sense of being known by and to a stranger whose fist was pushed inside his anus: a moment of "beautiful, painful coming together". My assumption was a misreading of what Tony needed from chemsex. It was not to meet his potential husband. It was to lose sight of himself, with all his agonising memories, his terribly shrunken sense of self, and his terror of intimacy. It was so much safer for him to hide himself in the grip of a group of others than to find himself with just one man, a man who might actually dare to see him.

Once I let go of my wish to transform Tony's stories of anonymous sex into a redemptive tale of the search for love, it became easier to decode the other unconscious motivations underpinning his compulsions. Shame lay beneath it all. He had been forced to reject the world of relational sex because he could not conceive of himself as someone that anyone would wish to relate to. The world of chemsex offered him a form of psychic annihilation in which the weight of his history could be jettisoned in favour of a world where sexual gratification was instantaneous and free from the pressure of being known. For him it was also possible to achieve a form of mastery over the trauma of his abuse. The aggression and hatred he felt towards his grandmother could be enacted in his sexual transactions; he could hate his partners without there ever being any consequences.

Over time it became more possible for me to say some of this and for Tony to hear some of it. The dawning of an understanding did, eventually, provide Tony with relief from his compulsion, although there was an agonising delay between insight and action. For a long time he voiced the despair he felt at knowing why he was caught up in such self-destructive behaviours while continuing to be addicted to them. I lost track of the number of sessions I spent alone, wondering where Tony had got to, whether he was lost in another bout of sexual acting out, or whether he was stuck in his bedroom, unable to face the thought of coming to the consulting room to face his history. When he eventually returned he would describe how after our last session he had felt stronger and more able to loosen the grip his addictions had on him, but how, within a few days he was magnetically pulled by his computer, adhesively bonded to the internet, his fingers continually clicking on images that were incrementally more perverse and more compulsive. It was as if he was Alice falling into Wonderland, unable to stop plummeting downwards, unsure of where he would land, finding himself back in a room with strangers, desperately seeking refuge from pain through immersion in drugs and anonymous sex.

I realised that Tony's feverish compulsions seemed to worsen following sessions in which we discussed his abuse, confirming my sense that his compulsion was anaesthetic in nature. It served to numb him from the pain of memory while simultaneously reheating the trauma within him. In the end he broke down, missing a month of sessions as the full weight of his despair overwhelmed him. When he returned his voice seemed deader than ever, and he talked of wishing to end the therapy, claiming that it was making him worse rather than better. I reflected on the potential disaster of his decision and how alone it could leave him. While affirming that the decision would ultimately be his, a decision he was fully entitled to make, I made it clear that I was concerned for his safety should he end therapy prematurely. This seemed to help contain his terror, and he agreed to continue. In retrospect it is clear that his breakdown and attempted severing of our therapeutic connection represented a turning point for him, as he seemed more able to examine his trauma without immediately plunging back into the world of chemsex afterwards. Gradually, he began to use the internet not simply to arrange an arid, non-relational sexual encounter or to subject himself to yet more images of objectless sex, but to strike up potential relationships, to connect with others in a non-perverse, relational way. He was able to view others as people rather than as objects, and to see sex as an emotional union rather than as a dry and lifeless way of expelling his self-hatred into another. It was a long process that included its fair share of disappointments for us both, times when the pull of his compulsions overwhelmed him and, following a period of significant therapeutic progress, he would disappear back into his chemsex retreat. These periods did, over time, become less frequent, and he seemed increasingly able to transfer his attachment needs from unknown men to me and, ultimately, to a sexual partner with whom his narrative could be shared.

* * *

Sexual compulsion is for many male survivors a hunger that can never be sated, a life-changing traumatogenic symptom that uses the guise of sexual excitement and gratification to rob the survivor of joy, true desire, and fulfilment. Sex for such patients is transformed from a reciprocal, loving exchange into a narcissistic, one-sided objectification of the other. The aim of a sexual encounter thus becomes primarily concerned with sensation rather than feeling. It becomes embedded within the unconscious, a dysfunctional but horribly addictive way of anaesthetising psychic pain. Those stuck in this joyless cycle of pseudo-excitement inevitably come to therapy with deeply engrained ambivalence. The desire to change the symptom is in conflict with the desire to retain its secondary gains. Already the transference is a complex one: the therapist oscillating between idealised helper who can rid the patient of his agonies and punishing depriver, interested only in divesting the patient of the one thing that affords him a sense of life.

Repetition compulsion

Tony's case is a far from an unusual one, and is, indeed, one we can see echoes of through the development of psychoanalytic thinking on the notions of addiction and compulsion. Freud's interest in repetition compulsion was first noted in "Remembering, repeating and working through" (Freud, 1914g), and further explored in "Beyond the pleasure principle" (Freud, 1920g), leading to a view of compulsive behaviour as an attempt to gain mastery over early trauma. In Tony's case the trauma was multifaceted, and it would be too simplistic to conclude that his sexual compulsion was solely a response to his grandmother's abusive actions. Through my work with him I came to recognise the weight and impact of his mother's illness, and her perceived abandonment of him. The original trauma may be defined in object-relational terms as a failure of care that results in others being experienced as objects rather than multifaceted human beings.

Drive theory views sexual compulsion as a maladaptive response to early developmental difficulties that render the adult unable to form a compromise between individual instinctual wishes and external societal demands. Another view is that of trauma theory that characterises sexual compulsion as a symptom of the emptiness felt by the patient who distances himself from the demands of emotional life in order to cope with the pain of life experiences. Van der Kolk felt there was "no evidence to support Freud's idea that repetition eventually leads to mastery and resolution" (1989, p. 399). He noted that some traumatised people remain preoccupied with trauma at the expense of other life experiences, and "have a vague sense of apprehension, emptiness, boredom and anxiety when not involved in activities reminiscent of the trauma" (p. 399). This description fits uncannily with the notes I made following my first session with Tony, in which I attempted to describe the strong countertransference response that was lodged in me, one of despair and hopelessness, which made me wonder whether psychotherapy would have any impact upon him. This was, of course, long before glimpses of his pathologies and the traumatogenic reasons for them began to emerge.

History of sexual compulsion

Tony's symptoms have a longer clinical history. Krafft-Ebbing described the seemingly modern phenomenon of sexual compulsion over 130 years ago;

> in which a person's sexual appetite is abnormally increased and permeates all his thoughts and feelings, allowing of no other aims in life, tumultuously, and in a rut-like fashion demanding gratification without granting the possibility of moral and righteous counter-presentations, and resolving itself into an impulsive, insatiable succession of sexual enjoyments. (1886, p. 70)

Whether sexually compulsive behaviour should be described as addictive is a contentious issue. Carnes (1983) suggests that the presence of the following three factors is necessary in order to formulate a diagnosis of sexual addiction:

1. Loss of control, demonstrated by unsuccessful attempts to regulate the behaviour.
2. Continuation of the behaviour despite adverse consequences.
3. Obsession or preoccupation with using or not using the behaviour.

All these factors were very much alive in Tony's treatment, alongside Goodman's (1992) characterisation of sexual addiction as a form of behaviour that can function both to produce pleasure and to provide escape from internal discomfort. This neatly encapsulates the double bind in which Tony found himself. An ever present yearning for an elusive sense of satisfaction and an attachment object that functioned in a sadomasochistic way to continually deny him the relief that masturbation and sex seemed to promise.

Reed and Blaine (1988) formulated a four-phase description of sexual compulsion, incorporating:

i. a phase of obsession, during which in response to existential and/or traumatogenic difficulties the subject is totally absorbed by sexual preoccupations;

ii. a phase of ritualisation, during which the subject executes rituals that precede sexual behaviour;
iii. a phase of sexual activity, which leads to a temporary and provisory relief;
iv. a phase of despair, underpinned by an awareness of the incapacity to control one's own behaviour.

Sexual promiscuity offers a temporary relief for anxiety, insecurity, and depression that is comparable to chemical drug dependency (Hatfield, 1988). Walsh's (1995) study found that subjects who reported weak parental attachment were more involved in sexually compulsive behaviour (and exhibited more drug use) than subjects who reported stronger parental attachment. Gartner describes sexually compulsive behaviour as "a dissociative solution to the problem of managing anxiety" (1999, p. 165), and argues that sexually addictive behaviours can be ways of controlling other more self-destructive or aggressive impulses. While it is clear that this is not a purely masculine phenomenon, it is striking that eighty per cent of subjects treated for sexual addictions are men (Estellon & Mouras, 2012). At the heart of Tony's pathologies lay a murderous rage that was too easily projected into himself or into his sexual partners. The constant thirst for sexual experiences may also serve the function of recapitulating the survivor's original lesson that the only way to experience closeness or perceived "love" is through sex. Compulsive re-enactments of the original trauma are relived in attempts to control the out-of-control; thus trauma coding begins the addictive cycle (Giugliano, 2006).

Rado (1957) linked the compulsive nature of addiction with the concepts of libidinal and pleasure principles. Hypersexuality, as described by Giugliano (2006), is:

> libidinal energy that finds no outlet in genital activity and therefore produces neurotic symptoms, inner restlessness, and a disturbance in the capacity for work and love. Inadequate orgasm is followed by unpleasant tension. When sexual activity fails to relieve the damming of libidinal energy, more tension is generated, and so on. Compulsions can be seen as automatic but inappropriate attempts to find an outlet for infantile instinctual tensions, of which the ego carries out the actions without conscious understanding of the meaning. (1996, p. 279)

Paraphilic and non-paraphilic compulsions

It is important, both for ourselves as clinicians and, sometimes, for our patients, to hold in mind a separation between what Coleman (1992) delineated as paraphilic and non-paraphilic compulsions. First, the paraphilic, involving unconventional sexual behaviours in which there is a disturbance in the object of sexual gratification or in the expression of sexual gratification. Second, the non-paraphilic, in which ordinary sexual behaviours have become addictive and, consequently, uncontrollable. Tony represents a case of the paraphilic, in so far as there had never been for him the notion of an ordinary, reciprocal, non-traumatic sexual encounter. While psychotherapy undoubtedly afforded him much relief from the grip of his compulsions, it is fair to say that he had to continue to work hard, once his therapy had ended, to regulate a strong gravitation towards the perverse. The disturbance in his sexual axis was early, and perpetrated by a strong attachment figure. Both factors make it quantifiably more difficult to maintain a sense of the sexually ordinary—the goal of Tony's therapy, and of his life. In many ways he conformed to what Joyce McDougall (1992) described in her essential work *Plea for a Measure of Abnormality*, where she described patients obsessed by sex as being "slaves of quantity". A beautiful but terribly poignant description that conveys a deep sense that Tony held of enslavement to his symptoms.

The way in which Tony was able to detail comprehensively the minutiae of his abuse without any tangible affect in his voice or demeanour resonated for me with Crowder's (1995) findings as to the ways in which men differ from women in their reporting of traumatic memory. He found that men had a propensity to dissociate from emotions while women were more dissociated from the cognitive details of their abuse. As with most gendered findings, we should not conclude that this applies equally to all men and all women. My practice has included some men whose ability to connect with their feelings about trauma far outweighs their capacity to recall the details of the trauma itself.

Difficulties with time

While Tony's difficulties with managing time decreased somewhat towards the end of our work, they reminded me of a part of his pathology that I feared would remain resistant to my attempts to interpret and understand. Kernberg (2008) described how problematic a healthy relationship with time is for patients with narcissistic pathologies, including those who, like Tony, are consumed by a narcissistic libido. Tony's relationship with time had a deeply subjective quality, coloured by his psychological state. Trauma had separated him from an objective, linear view of time, with his constant lateness not merely communicating either an unconscious hope that I would mourn his absence, or that I would feel the force of his aggressive rage towards me. It was also a profound symptom of the way in which trauma had removed from him a normal, ordinary relationship with time, much as a distorted relationship with temporality can occur in patients with severe dissociation (Auerbach, 2014).

One important aspect of Tony's presentation to note is the state of his non-sexual relationships. He was a "man's man". Into his highly pressurised schedule of pornographic masturbation and round-the-clock encounters with multiple sexual partners he managed to maintain a group of male friends, mostly work colleagues. He spoke with some pride about this part of his life, congratulating himself on his capacity to manage such friendships despite his history and despite his many symptoms of trauma. What became clear over time, however, was how closely these friendships mirrored Tony's objectified, chemically enhanced sexual encounters. These were friends with whom he shared next to nothing about his personal life and around whom he formed tight, boundaried parameters. Friendship for him conformed more to the contemporary social media concept, the world of Facebook and Twitter, where people can think of themselves as "friends" without ever having met. These colleagues were people who, it could be argued, had never actually encountered the real Tony. They knew and seemed to like the false self persona that he had constructed over the years, but it is doubtful that any authentic intimacy existed within these friendships.

Splitting and the fear of intimacy

Splitting tends to be the main defence used by those engaged in sexual compulsions. As Estellon and Mouras write: "Its main aim is to avoid the confrontation of the subject, in the face of his affective ambivalence, with depressive suffering. Here, splitting radically separates affectionate impulses from sexual impulses. Sexual partners will be little invested affectively, whereas other people in the entourage (friends, family, inaccessible partner) are highly invested" (Estellon & Mouras, 2012, p. 8). Khan (1981) compared sexual compulsion to a drug fix, its function being to provide an escape from pain, rage, depression, or paralysing apathy. The sexual act is a painfully incomplete one because his sexual partner is never experienced as a real person. There is no reciprocity and therefore no real pleasure. Sexual compulsion was, for Tony, a way of avoiding intimacy. Addiction to pornography had provided him with a psychic retreat (Steiner, 2004), a place in which sexual needs could be gratified without having to deal with the overwhelming demands of others. Through this form of narcissistic omnipotence, Tony kept the complexities of others at bay, achieving a self-soothing form of protection that acted as a protective membrane against those intrusive memories of abuse that continually threatened to attack his sense of self.

Resistance to improvement

Working with patients whose lives have been consumed by sexual compulsion requires a capacity to analyse the aetiology of the compulsion and provide an alternative to it. We have to expect significant resistance from patients. Our attempts to wean them off their compulsion will be experienced as a form of attack, touching on early experiences of deprivation. The patient can too easily feel like the baby being deprived of the breast. Sexual compulsion is, as we have seen, an escape from intimacy. It also holds a perverse excitement that we need to acknowledge—the patient's attachment to their symptom has to be benignly understood. In order to convey a sense of holding and containment, I had to provide Tony with an experience of his compulsion being understood. It was unhelpful to prematurely pathologise and interpret the components of the sexually addictive life he led. I had to show I understood that for him it was not the horror movie it often seemed to me to be. It was also exciting, colourful and enervating. If it is conceptualised through interpretation as merely a malign symptom, the patient will resist any attempts to loosen its symptomatic grip. This can provoke a long period of inertia. The patient will need to share repeatedly the details of the compulsion in perverse and mind-numbing detail. Such accounts can flood the therapist in a form of psychic attack that renders thought and insight difficult to attain or sustain. The urge may be to dissociate or to prematurely interpret, seeking to place meaning on the compulsion. To do this too quickly is a mistake. The patient needs to feel that he and his compulsion are understood before an alternative way of processing early trauma can be expressed and internalised.

The inevitable breakdown

The point at which the nature of the defensive compulsion is realised can coincide with or provoke a form of breakdown. Once the defence mechanism is understood as a dysfunctional symptom, the patient can experience an overwhelming sense of despair. The compulsion has become concretised, functioning as a dam holding back the tide of early trauma. Once the dam is removed the patient can feel as if he is drowning. Care must be taken in all areas of treatment. At point of initial assessment the therapist must examine what form of support is available to the patient. At point of breakdown the therapist will need to be able to liaise with the patient's GP, social worker, or whatever support person has been identified. I see this as providing a dual sense of containment—for the therapist as much as for the patient.

Working with sexual addiction necessitates a long and slow treatment process (Goodman, 1992; Craparo, 2011; Estellon & Mouras, 2012). We are working with an attachment to a symptom that has provided the patient with years of comfort, validation, and excitement. It is likely that one compulsion will sit alongside others, occupying a place within a complex web of addictions. Carnes et al. (2005) found that the following addictions stood alongside sexual compulsivity in their male subjects (in descending order of frequency): alcoholism, substance abuse, caffeine addiction, compulsive working, high-risk behaviour, compulsive spending, nicotine, compulsive eating, compulsive violence, addictive athleticism, compulsive hoarding, compulsive cleaning, compulsive gambling, and food. Each addiction or compulsion may feed off and reinforce another, coming as they often do from the same aetiology. Huebner (1993), writing from a neuroscientific perspective, includes deprivation in his overview of addictions, and notes the similarities between patients at extreme ends of the addiction spectrum. Family therapists have observed how addictions and compulsions become part of a family's systemic functioning. A wife's overeating, for example, interacts with her husband's alcoholism, and both interact with their son's drug addiction. It is rare for a compulsion to exist in isolation.

Premature termination of treatment

Given the complex interweaving of compulsive symptomology and our patients' strong attachments to their addictions, we should not be surprised that many patients terminate their treatment prematurely. The cost of recovery is often too high a price to pay, the perverse pull of sexualised comfort proving far more seductive than the challenge of treatment. Most therapists are familiar with the flight into health undertaken by the patient who chooses to leave just before a moment of mutative growth, and the dreadful feelings of impotence, frustration, and loss we are left with. There are patients for whom the time is not yet right, whose premature departure of treatment represents a pause in their treatment rather than a termination. There are others for whom the tug of pathology is too powerful, who have to project into us their ongoing sense of hopelessness. Their addiction is not just sexual, it is an addiction to despair.

Craparo (2011) considers sexual compulsion to be a form of dissociative self-medication for a body injured by memories of recurring traumatic experiences stored in the somatic memory. Weaning the patient off this strong and potent brand of self-medication requires the fostering of an understanding and re-attunement of the patient's relationship with pain. Craparo (2014) considers this in terms of mentalisation-based therapy, although I think the distinctions between this and the work of relational, insight-based psychodynamic psychotherapy are exaggerated. We do with the sexual compulsive what we do with most patients tormented by their symptoms: we forge links between their pain and their history through interpretation, making use of the transference and countertransference as best we can. The work with Tony required a gradual peeling away of the layers surrounding his early developmental history. His traumata were connected by loss (of his mother), perversion (by his grandmother), and absence (of his father). The invisibility of his father was something he had never dared to think about before his therapy, the weight of this absence serving to further blur his capacity to identify with one gender or the other. There was, at times in my work with him, a paternal feel to the transference, with me often taking up a quasi-fatherly tone in my interpretations and interventions. Tony himself struggled at first to dare admit that this transference was taking place. His relating to me as a son relates to a father, imagined, in his case, triggered immense feelings of loss for the father he had never had.

This father was sometimes idealised, cherished, and loved. At other times he was hated, abhorred, his importance denigrated and denied. All of this was played out in the transference between us, with his view of me oscillating between idealisation and denigration, before finally arriving at a place somewhere between the two.

Eventual enlivenment

It was helpful to monitor how Tony's slow disengagement from the world of chemsex and his tentative exploration of the world of reciprocal, mutual relationships coincided with an injection of life into the ways in which he described himself. His voice gained some colour in his final year of therapy, transforming from the flat, lifeless tone he had maintained for most to his life to a voice that was actually capable of communicating emotion—both positive and negative. This coincided with something new for Tony, an interest in life and in the possibility that a relationship could be devoid of abuse and exploitation. As has been demonstrated through Tony's case, sexual compulsions are often a way of anaesthetising the agony of shame. For many male survivors the prospect of intimacy contains within it the threat of psychic annihilation. Relationships are to be avoided because they are Trojan horses containing menace and danger. Sexual abuse has attacked the ability to conceptualise sex as a normal, creative, and fulfilling phenomenon. Sex becomes primarily about sensation rather than emotion. It also becomes a forum in which hatred and aggression can be expelled without any obvious consequences. Partners can be hated because they do not matter in the first place. Psychotherapy with sexually compulsive men involves the replacement of the perverse with the healthy, but to facilitate such a transformation requires time and the capacity on the therapist's part to withstand a form of immersion into the patient's world of non-relational, drug-fuelled encounters, a world that can seem alien, alarming, arousing, frightening, and seductive.

It is rare for an authentic process of change to occur for the patient without some form of breakdown taking place, such is the power of the grip of perverse defences that have usually dominated the patient for many years. Working with sexual compulsion involves encounters with an extreme form of narcissism that has been magnified by perverse excitement and gratification, a version of repetition compulsion that we should remember is not purely psychological. The infusion of drugs provides a physiological dimension to the patient's pathology, making the therapeutic process a doubly complex challenge in which both mind and body have become enthralled to addictions. It is rare for such compulsions to have their genesis solely in experiences of sexual trauma. The deeper and longer we work with patients the more likely we are to uncover disturbances in early object-relational histories that require attending to. While sexual abuse may be the most vividly prominent cause for compulsion, we must be vigilant for signs of a basic fault (Balint, 1979) in the patient's early history that may account for the profound difficulties many patients encounter in their struggle to achieve a capacity for healthy relatedness.

We must also expect there to be significant ruptures in our work. The addicted patient will resist attempts to wean him off his drugs of choice, and will be bound to vanish from his treatment at moments of despair or, more usually, at points in the therapy where he may be starting to feel some hope. At times the patient will be torn between two different breasts, one promising the familiar chemically induced, sexually enlivening bliss of his addiction, the other promising a route to healthier ways of relating to the world. For some the idea of being weaned off the addictive breast represents too painful a change to his internal world and he will engineer a flight into health, abandoning the therapist rather than abandoning his primary love. We have to expect that some patients will vanish. Other patients will return and, over time, the frequency of vanishings should diminish. We should also expect that when one compulsion is processed, understood, and worked through, another may take its place, with such changes in symptomology occurring until the patient's object-relational disturbances have been thoroughly worked through in the transference. As in so much of our work with male survivors, the transference is key to a process of internal change, with the therapist/patient dyad ultimately providing a template for a secure and intimate relationship, a safe alternative to the world of dangerous, but addictive, anonymity.

CHAPTER FOUR

There is no such thing as a survivor: forensic psychotherapy and the abused/abuser split

"I feel desperate. I'm going to do something. I think I've done something already. Not abused a child. Touched, maybe. I thought it was in the past but it won't go away. The only option left is to kill myself; I know that. Kill myself before I do something."

These terrifying words were spoken by "Nawaz" in his first session with me. He had been referred by his GP, to whom he had made similarly chilling statements. Nawaz was in his mid-twenties, an ordinary, fairly nondescript-looking man who had struggled to attain the success yearned for him by his strict Muslim parents. He had dropped out of university in his first year and had taken to staying with friends for a few months at a time, usually until their patience with his slovenly, unhygienic habits broke. He was, at the time of referral, back living with his parents, who had given him a time limit of six months to get a job, otherwise they would evict him once more. He had never had an adult sexual relationship, and described himself as one of "life's losers—there's no one out there for me. Who on earth would have me?"

It was easy to see how Nawaz tried the patience of those who tried so hard to support him. His attendance at sessions was sporadic and he was often late, citing his forgetfulness or his having overslept. Despite his opening plea for help, he seemed, at best, ambivalent about working for it. He lasted a year with me before agreeing to be referred to a specialist forensic clinic, and in that year managed to instil in me a vivid sense of what it must be like to be him. I found myself invaded and colonised by his ambivalence. Despite the severity of his symptoms and the compelling child protection concerns he presented, I struggled to care much about him. He was seeing a probation officer at the same time he was attending his sessions with me, so I felt unrealistically reassured that there was a support network out there for him when he decided to abandon the safety net I was trying to construct. There were moments in sessions when I was terrified by his sexual fantasies, particularly those involving young children, and yet there were also times when he reduced me to near-sleep. He could speak hypnotically about the minutiae of his day in a numbing, soporific way, to the point where I had to internally pinch myself to stay alive in the session with him.

This phenomenon was at its height when he began to disclose the details of his own experiences of having been sexually abused by his mother's brother. He told me about how, when he was five, his uncle would take him for treats after mosque, to places his parents would probably have disapproved of—the cinema, amusement arcades, fast food joints—places he quickly understood he could not tell them he had visited. From this it was not a huge leap to remain silent about the times his uncle would touch him while watching a film, the touching becoming incrementally more assertive, culminating in masturbation and oral assault in visits to his uncle's house. The abuse continued until Nawaz was seventeen, at which point he threatened to report his uncle to the police. He had told no one else, apart from his GP, about what had happened.

There was a curious and disturbing undercurrent to the way in which Nawaz described his uncle's abuse. He would recount it with the same uninterested, lethargic tone with which he discussed his efforts to clean his room or his latest interview at the Jobcentre. "It just happened," he would say, disinterestedly. "It seemed, I don't know, sort of inevitable that it did … I suppose it was upsetting, but I don't remember being that upset." I struggled to comprehend Nawaz's lack of passion, a dearth of affect that touched so many areas of his life. The dramatic opening to his work with me, his searingly honest declaration of his fears of being a sexual abuser, was not sustained. Months passed before he mentioned these fears once more, and in the meantime I had found myself almost imagining that I had fantasised the whole disclosure, so absent had it become from our work. When it was mentioned once more it was with his familiar lethargy and dispassion. He told me that he had seen his GP, who had voiced his hope that he had been talking with me about his sexual risk. "Not that it's a problem at the moment," he said, seeking to both reassure me and fend me off. "I mean, I did wonder about my thoughts, but I suppose most people do, at some point." It came as a surprise to him that I considered these thoughts worthy of more examination, that most people did not, in fact, harbour sexual thoughts about children, and that I was more interested in his anxieties than his reassurance.

Nawaz related to me with a marked lack of interest. He lived within a narcissistic shell, my efforts to examine his curiosity about me or about others in his life coming to nothing. In response to my wondering whether he wondered about me, what I made of him, what thoughts I held in my mind about the thoughts in his, he declared that I was a closed book to him, a book he was not inclined to open. "I mean, you seem to want me to talk about what I feel about you. But I feel nothing, really." And yet my breaks were preceded and followed by a barrage of questions about where I was holidaying and who with. He remarked on when my hair was cut, or whether I was wearing a new item of clothing. He rejected my attempts to interpret his curiosity, stating instead that he was simply being polite, respecting normal social etiquette. This oscillation between interest and disdain had a curious effect on me, leaving me perpetually unsure of whether there was a real, dynamic relationship between us or whether I was in the presence of a carefully constructed false self. The break, with its associations with loss and abandonment, did seem to impinge on his solipsistic view of the world.

Our work only really came to life when I dared to challenge his denial. I took the risk of letting him know that I considered our first session as being the only time when he had felt brave enough to show me his real self, largely because of his unconscious assumption that I would be so repelled that I would refuse to work with him. I interpreted his terror of being known and his fear of his real sexual feelings being revealed and looked at. This shook Nawaz, and he found himself having to acknowledge something real and tangible in our work. Eventually he began to tell me that his sexual thoughts had not, in fact, gone away, but were as frequent and as terrifying as ever. In the sessions leading up to his referral elsewhere, he dared to tell me more about dreams he had involving children, how he had "found himself" gravitating towards school playgrounds, desperate for a sight of children. He eventually disclosed his heavy use of pornography, and his addiction to viewing images of children being sexually abused. He struggled to understand this in the context of his own abuse, and swayed between bewilderment that the acts that had caused him such harm now had such a strong grip on him, and a tacit understanding that he was drawn to these images as a perverse way of understanding the pain he had undergone.

As I was seeing Nawaz in private practice I had to conclude that the intimacy of our sessions was too much for him to bear. In truth, it was too much for me to bear as well. Welldon (1993, 1996b, 2011) speaks about the need for forensic psychotherapy to take place in a triangular context, and highlights the dangers of such intensive clinical work taking place without the protective membrane of a safe and secure institution. In ascertaining Nawaz's capacity to be seen in private practice it was, however, not simply the absence of clinical line management, psychiatric involvement, and robust child protection protocols that I had to consider. There was something deeply frightening about him and his sexual fantasies that impacted on my eventual conclusion that he had to be seen within the confines of a specialist clinic. Fortunately, his GP was able to facilitate this, an increasingly difficult process given both the paucity of specialist settings and the lack of health funding to underwrite such referrals.

In working with male survivors, it will not always be as clear as it was in Nawaz's case that the patient is a forensic one. Without the referral signposting undertaken by his GP, it is possible that I would have begun to see him, as I do so many patients, thinking of him primarily as a survivor rather than a potential perpetrator. This is a mistake as it involves taking up a narrow, split view of human sexuality. To presume that no survivors will present forensic symptoms is as naive and misguided as presuming that all will. To paraphrase Winnicott's (1960) dictum that there is no such thing as just an infant, there is no such thing as just a survivor. There is always a survivor in relation to his abuser. It is not only the horror of abuse—its bodily sensations, its psychic annihilation—that is internalised by the survivor, it is the abuser too. What the survivor then does with this introject is pivotal to the relationship he will have with trauma through the rest of his life.

* * *

From abused to abuser

Only a minority of male survivors become perpetrators of sexual abuse, and yet the fear of becoming an abuser tends to be a preoccupation for many—both survivors and those around them. These anxieties stem partly from misconceptions about gendered responses to sexual abuse: the assumption, as reported by Carmen et al. (1984), that male victims direct their reactions to abuse externally, female victims internally. While this may be true, it should not read as an indicator of a disposition towards sexualised aggression. The true picture is a far more complex one. Salter et al. (2003) conducted a longitudinal study of 224 former male victims of sexual abuse. Of these, twenty-six had subsequently committed sexual offences, in almost all cases with children, mainly outside their families. The study concluded that most male victims of child sexual abuse do not become paedophiles, and, in focusing on the minority in their group who did, identified those factors that seemed to increase the risk of victims becoming abusers in later life. These included neglect, lack of supervision, and sexual abuse by a woman or girl. Those victims who did go on to abuse had also more frequently witnessed serious intrafamilial violence than those who did not. While other studies have suggested a consistent association between child sexual abuse and higher rates of sexual risk behaviours—particularly sex trading, more sexual partners, and an earlier age of first intercourse—Senn et al. (2008) question these findings. The failure to arrive at a consistent definition of child sexual abuse, failure to investigate gender as a moderator, and possible confounding of the child sexual abuse experience with some of the sexual behaviour outcome variables, serve to weaken the conclusion that the association between abuse and abusing is causal.

In their review of 843 patients attending a specialist forensic psychotherapy clinic, Glasser et al. (2001) found that among the 747 males the overall rate of having been a victim was thirty-five per cent for perpetrators and eleven per cent for non-perpetrators. Of the ninety-six females studied, forty-three per cent had experienced sexual abuse while only one was a perpetrator. A high percentage of male subjects abused by a female relative (most commonly a sister or a mother) became perpetrators, with parental loss in childhood also being a strong predictor of being a perpetrator.

As noted in the preceding chapter, Freud's concept of repetition compulsion (1914g) may be understood in the context of traumatic repetitions as an attempt to retrospectively master the original trauma. In the case of the survivor, it also becomes an attempt to recast the trauma, with the victim taking on the role of perpetrator as a way of relieving himself from the unbearable feelings of powerlessness, impotence, and terror that come with victimhood. Van der Kolk (1989) underscores the destructiveness of the repetition compulsion, which has the reverse effect of its unconscious motivation—causing ongoing suffering for the self and for others. Ferenczi introduced the concept of "identification with the aggressor" in his groundbreaking "Confusion of tongues" paper (1949). Howell (2014) describes how identification with the aggressor can be understood as a two-stage process. The first stage is automatic and initiated by trauma, but the second stage is defensive and purposeful. While identification with the aggressor begins as an automatic organismic process, with repeated activation and use it gradually becomes a defensive process. Broadly, as a dissociative defence, it has two enacted relational parts: the part of the victim and the part of the aggressor.

Somatisation of abuse

The survivor's fear of offending far outweighs both probability and possibility. Despite evidence to the contrary, it appears to be difficult for many survivors to rid themselves of a terror that they are caught in a cycle of abuse and abusing. This is partly due to some of the responses to sexual abuse being encoded in the body, provoking physical reactions that are both confusing and disturbing to the survivor. While sexual abuse is predominantly an act of power and aggression, it is also sexual. It is, on the whole, a bodily attack involving physiological as much as psychological responses. For a child, or, for that matter, an adult, there is something deeply perplexing about how a body responds to attack. It may freeze, shut down, or retaliate. It may also find itself becoming excited. Survivors often report two horrific realisations when reflecting on the impact of abuse upon them: that at the time of abuse they may have had an erection and, in some cases, may have ejaculated; and that in looking back on the abuse they may find themselves holding feelings of retrospective arousal. Part of the work of psychotherapy is to help survivors process the various ways in which abuse can be embodied and somatised. This therapeutic territory is strewn with potential explosions, as attempts by the therapist to normalise feelings of arousal felt by the patient can be experienced as attempts to pathologise, to somehow conflate arousal and aggression. This is especially problematic when aspects of the abuse have become fetishised to the point of perverse ritualisation.

Psychotherapeutic work with male survivors can require something of a psycho-educative component when working with the patient's fears of abusing. How this is worked with depends on whether the patient's fears are anxiety-based or reality-based.

Anxiety-based fears of abusing

Patients in this category hold a fear of abusing that is at odds with their actual level of risk. When examining their anxieties they tend to focus not just on the impact upon themselves of becoming an abuser, they will also be able to explore the impact upon possible future victims. Through this they demonstrate a level of empathy that tends to be unavailable to patients who present a real risk of offending. As such, they may need a level of normative, psycho-educative input that reinforces the relatively low incidence of survivors going on to abuse children. Without this, it may be difficult for the patient to be able to then examine their physiological and psychological responses to sexual excitement and arousal without feeling overwhelmed by their fears of re-enactment.

Reality-based fears of abusing

Such patients will tend to describe their fears of abusing in narcissistic ways, voicing their fear of getting in trouble, losing their relationship, or being identified by others as an abuser. When prompted to conjecture on the possible impact on victims, the patient may struggle to voice an authentically empathic reaction. Victims will be conceptualised as part-objects or as extensions of the patient's self. For such patients a psycho-educative approach will be counterproductive, serving to reinforce and magnify their capacity to dissociate from and deny their levels of sexual risk. Instead the therapist will have to ascertain what level of danger the patient presents, before they can calibrate what level of therapeutic intervention will be suitable to help address his underlying pathology.

Assessing risk and danger

Evaluating how dangerous a patient is cannot be conducted in isolation. Risk assessment is a systemic process that requires more than one lens through which a pathology can be examined. The first port of call for the therapist will be his or her clinical supervisor, but if the supervisor is not forensically experienced external consultation should be accessed. An integrated approach is needed in order to ascertain, amongst other things, past history of abuse, levels of sexual and non-sexual aggression, and presence of psychosis (Doctor, 2003). The therapist attempting on his or her own to evaluate perverse psychopathology in a patient is vulnerable to a wide range of projections, cognitive distortions, and minimisations. Most particularly we are vulnerable to perverse splitting. The forensic patient has an investment in our continuing to see him purely as a victim. If a strong therapeutic alliance has been constructed, altering this view in any significant way can be impossible without external help. In some ways it requires the building of a quasi-organisational structure, mirroring the institutional triangulation that is the optimum clinical setting for forensic psychotherapy.

Dangers of working in private practice

The psychotherapist who finds him or herself working with a sexually dangerous patient has a series of questions to answer before feeling able to continue with the work. First, do you wish to continue? This is not simply a question of whether forensic patients should be seen in private practice. It is an important question about the agency we feel we have to accept or refuse certain types of patient. Working with male survivors happens because of a certain interest in sexual trauma, abuse, and masculinity. It may feed our curiosity about the impact of sexual violation upon the male psyche. It may touch on our own experiences of hurt and damage. We may need to work to feed our own narcissistic, altruistic needs. Working with sexual abusers represents stepping into a fundamentally different territory. I believe in a non-split view of sexual aggression. I work with the victim within the victimiser and strive not to divide my patients into good victims and evil abusers. Such a split is clinically unhelpful. Yet working with men who are at risk of enacting the most appalling sexual fantasies involving children should not be something we are compelled to do, and stating one's desire to not do this should not be regarded as a personal and professional failing. It is, for some, a rational and sensible response to the enormous power of forensic work to get under our skin, to contaminate our thoughts and feelings about sex, children, desire, and perversion. Deciding to refer a patient on is an enormous decision and we have to be mindful of the impact upon our patients of any act that can so vividly reconnect them with experiences of abandonment and loss. There are times, however, when such decisions are vital for the safety of both patient and therapist.

The core complex

Working with forensic patients requires a clear map with which to negotiate the complexities of perverse psychopathologies. I have written previously on working forensically with patients with intellectual disabilities (Corbett, 2014), making particular use of Glasser's (1979) concept of the core complex. This theory is equally helpful in considering the therapeutic needs of male survivors who have acted out sexually, as it contextualises the forensic patient's perverse actions in early object relations. Glasser contextualised fears of annihilation and intimacy within early deprivation and neglect, and observed the playing out of this psychopathology in adult life in the forensic patient's manic oscillation between closeness with and distance from others. The core of Glasser's complex is a fear of intimacy, a need to keep the object of sexual desire both close and at bay, and to treat it sadistically. The forensic patient is characterised by thin-skinned narcissism (Rosenfeld, 1987), stemming from the infantile experience of the mother (or primary carer) as being potentially overwhelming and destructive. The patient thus has a seemingly unsolvable dilemma. He has a "deep-seated and pervasive longing for an intense and most intimate closeness to another person, amounting to a 'merging', a 'state of oneness', 'a blissful union'" (Glasser, 1979, p. 278), and yet he cannot bear the terrifying, suffocating intimacy of what he wants. It has then to be retreated from, or destroyed.

Welldon's "circular motion of perversion" (1996a) posits sexual anxiety as emanating from the conflict between the id and the superego, and locates anxiety as being the motor of sexual perversion. The forensic patient has inevitable difficulties with how he relates to others. The concept of an equal, reciprocal, relational exchange is a tremendously difficult notion for the forensic patient to deal with. He tends not to be able to be think of another as a subject. Others are often not even objects. They are *part*-objects whose presence as potential relational human beings is suffocated by the patient's propensity to privilege his desires and feelings over those of anyone else. We can best understand this as a form of malignant narcissism. Weigert (1967) describes this as a regressive state involving denial and a distortion of reality, while Keogh (2011) views it as a psychic structure that underlies psychopathy. This involves an obfuscation of the need for relationship and a desire to coerce and control others (Meloy, 1992).

Inability to mourn

The inability to mourn is a key diagnostic feature of perversion, and I became aware of Nawaz's difficulties in this area as we approached the ending of our work together and the beginning of his work elsewhere. He understood the reasons for the referral to a specialist unit and was, in fact, deeply relieved that his perverse feelings had been recognised and taken seriously by me. What he struggled to access, however, were those feelings of sadness and regret that tend to emerge, in myriad forms, in the ending of a therapeutic partnership. For Nawaz the ending and the new beginning were experienced as a form of transaction, an emotionless transitioning from one person to the other. I found myself surprised (and narcissistically hurt) by how easily he left me, but was helpfully reminded of this relational lack being a fundamental part of his psychopathology. Nawaz needed his perversion to function as what I have previously called a form of "pseudo-skin" (Corbett, 2014, p. 13). Without it, he tended to retreat into a barren internal and external world in which he could just about maintain a sense of psychic homeostasis. His disengagement from the world was his attempt to insulate himself against a world he viewed as threatening, catastrophic, and overwhelming. At the heart of many of his defences was a terror of intimacy. As felt most vividly in the transference between he and I, Nawaz had little concept of a safe emotional distance between himself and others. He struggled to navigate the complexities of a reciprocal relationship, adopting instead a veneer of polished compliance and depthless sociability. His relief at our therapy ending was a relief at having survived potential annihilation. I had become an object that, much like most of his internal objects, threatened to suffocate or abandon him. I imagine that, if I had not referred him on, he would have either ended the therapy himself or retreated more and more into a non-relational, bland, and inauthentic dynamic with me. The truth behind his sexual fantasies could only begin to emerge once he knew that our relationship was finite.

The narcissism of perversion

Stoller (1975) thought of perversion as the erotic form of hatred, an expression of self-loathing that has to be evacuated and projected into victims of sexual aggression. This becomes a "triumph over tragedy", with the person experiencing revenge against his abuser alongside the illusion of mastery. The illusion of mastery comes through gaining erotic agency over what was once beyond his control. Perversion is a state of knowing and not knowing, a paradox in which self-hatred can coexist with a deeply embedded narcissism. Here I am talking about pathological narcissism. We all need to have some healthy measure of narcissism in order to protect us from having to "to live a whole lifetime with the fate of death haunting one's dreams" (Becker, 1997, p. 27). The narcissistic adult vacillates between an irrational overestimation of the self and irrational feelings of inferiority. He relates to the objects of his desire as if they are extensions of himself, his interest only existing if the object can meet his needs (Glasser, 1987). This perverse dynamic is inevitably played out in the transference, the therapist tending to be viewed in mercenary terms as an object who is valued primarily for what she can give the patient rather than how she can enable the patient to promote internal change himself. Bach describes working with a narcissistic patient as being like "talking into the wind or writing on the sand, only to have one's words effaced moments later by the waves … the patient either welcomes or resents the analyst's words … and frequently does not even register the actual content. A session which seems to have led to a certain understanding or experience of some kind may, 24 hours later, be totally forgotten" (1977, p. 209).

In his theory of "temporary indwelling" Kohut (1971) proposes that the therapist should empathically experience the world from the patient's point of view, allowing the patient a sense of being understood by another. Bromberg (1983) argues that *unmodified* psychoanalytic treatment is unsuited to deal with narcissistic disorders, and that we should attune to the grandiose claims of our patients with what Gedo described as "maximal tact and empathy ... any failure in this regard is inevitably followed by humiliation and outrage" (1977, p. 183). Rothstein linked poor ego strength with the narcissistic patient's difficulty in withstanding transference interpretations: "Interpretive attempts to facilitate a working through process can evoke psychotic regressions (and) serious acting-out, sometimes including rapid disruption of the working relationship" (1982, pp. 177–178).

Narcissistic patients have at the heart of their pathology a fundamental inability "to be both 'in the world' and 'separate from it' at the same time, without endangering the one internal structure they depend upon for a sense of identity—the grandiose self" (Bromberg, 1983, p. 183). They lack an individuated core identity, this most vital of developmental attainments being sabotaged by early object-relational failures, subsequent sexual abuse, or both. In order for this to be worked through and processed, we need to "keep a finger on the pulse of the patient's self-esteem" (ibid., p. 186) while carefully allowing the patient to experience us as good enough (Winnicott, 1953) objects who can relieve them of the weight of solipsistic grandiosity. No therapeutic change can happen until the patient has introjected and internalised the therapist as a healthy object. Once this has taken place we can flex our analytic muscles somewhat more, allowing interpretative work to unfold and more risks to be taken in looking at the patient's objectification of others as sexual objects existing only for his gratification.

This first stage of therapy can be a long and painful one, involving as it does the playing out of the patient's resistance to change. Months (and years) can go by in which the patient appears to be stuck helplessly in his narcissistic cocoon. We can feel as if we are being experienced as another victim of abuse—someone without thoughts, feelings or desires, whose sole purpose is to satisfy the perverse needs of the patient. It is difficult but essential to conceptualise this as a developmental stage, a process of reparation in which the deficits of early deprivation and later (or, indeed, concurrent) abuse are being played out, re-experienced and, ultimately, repaired.

While paedophiles and incest perpetrators both exhibit narcissism, this is more clearly seen in paedophilia. As Glasser et al. state:

> In incest the relationship is not so exclusively narcissistic: the interrelations of the whole family are involved and the abusive act, therefore, has a different impact. However, it should be noted that the incest perpetrator brushes aside the incest barrier while the paedophile usually does not ... The actual experience of being abused frequently plays the role of the final organiser of the perpetrator's orientation and personality ... the abuser's target age-group is usually limited to the age when he was himself abused. The abusive act is a traumatic one—however cooperative the victim might appear to be—and the change from being the passive victim to the active perpetrator, making use of the mechanism of identification with the aggressor, is the way in which some victims repeatedly attempt to master the trauma. (2001, p. 492)

Countertransference issues

The forensic patient is difficult to treat, and many are unable to make the developmental link from narcissism to reciprocity. Our capacity to examine this depends largely on what use we make of the countertransference, what feelings are stirred (or not) in us by our patients, and what these feelings may be communicating about a thawing out of the patient's frozen internal world. Work with patients such as Nawaz should not be undertaken in the absence of a safe and secure organisational structure. The therapist undertaking such work requires supervision that not only provides a layer of forensic understanding, but a place to which can be brought the despair, hopelessness, and fear that forensic work can engender. The therapist working with the perpetrator has to maintain a delicate balance between risk assessment and treatment. The former precedes the latter, but they also merge as the work unfolds, assessment being, at its heart, a fluid and dynamic process. Patients become more or less dangerous as they delve deeper into their unconscious processes. Aggression and rage can emerge as primitive defences are deconstructed, leaving the forensic patient face to face with the trauma they have previously striven to dissociate from. By stressing the importance of classical psychoanalytic notions such as identification with the aggressor and repetition compulsion, I am seeking to remind us of the long history that forensic psychotherapy has. Despite it really only flowering towards the end of the twentieth century because of the work of such pioneers as Welldon, Cox, and Glasser, the world of psychoanalysis has long accommodated the notion of trauma being enacted through violence and crime. The less we are drawn towards splitting good victims from bad abusers, the more therapeutic space we afford those men who live their lives in a perilous state between the two.

CHAPTER FIVE

On not knowing the colour of a patient's eyes: working with profound depression

My supervisor asks me, as she often does, what the patient I am describing looks like. I hesitate, realising that, even though I have been working with "Jamie" for some time, I feel unable to describe him. I make vague allusions to his height, the kind of clothes he wears, the timbre of his voice, but something is missing. I struggle, and my supervisor prompts me with more questions, questions I continue to struggle to answer. We identify it at the same moment, falling upon the element of his description that is missing. It is his eyes. I have no idea what colour they are. I am shocked at this realisation, and, as we talk more, I realise I have no memory of seeing his eyes. They tend to be adhesively fixed on the carpet, with occasional glances at the hands he knots together as he speaks.

I bring this awareness into the next session, and realise how crucial this lack of eye contact is to my struggle to work with Jamie. I dare to talk about it with him, wondering what makes it so hard for him to lock eyes with me, what does he fear he will see in me or, perhaps more pertinently, what does he fear I will see in him? Jamie is deeply depressed, perhaps one of the most profoundly depressed men I have worked with. I see him twice a week and have come to dread the mornings that begin with his shuffling into my consulting room. He is familiar with the unspoken rules of our work—that I will not prompt him at the start of the session, that we will allow silences to develop where they need to develop, that my role is to hear him, to make some interpretations, but not to advise or counsel him. Unlike other patients, he appears absolutely fine with these terms of engagement. His story of abuse is familiar in some of its component parts, while also being one of the most unsettling and disturbing stories I have heard. He is a child of incest, his parents being siblings. They themselves were abused by their parents and from an early age (perhaps since birth) Jamie was abused by both his father and his mother. His father died when Jamie was twelve, at which point the abuse perpetrated by his mother intensified, taking on more sadistic and violent elements. He ran away from home at the age of fourteen, eventually living on the streets and falling into prostitution for a number of years. Alongside this he developed a drug habit, occasionally falling into petty crime to help feed this addiction. It was in his mid-twenties that Jamie's life was changed by entering a drug treatment programme. In the course of this he disclosed his history of abuse for the first time. By his early thirties Jamie's life bore little resemblance to what had gone before. He had entered full-time education, lived in his own flat, and appeared, on the surface, to have put his troubles behind him. He faced a further onslaught of trauma when he was diagnosed as HIV-positive, a fact that hastened his entry into psychotherapy.

When I talk to Jamie about how hard he finds it to lock his eyes with mine, he appears surprised. "I didn't know that's what I was doing," he says, and I come to realise that how he relates to me is how he relates to the world: with his eyes lowered, never daring to look life in the eye. This is symptomatic of Jamie's main presenting symptom: his profound depression. Despite the changes he has made in his life, and the colossal journey he has made from a life shaped by abuse to one that appears to resemble some kind of normality, his life is overshadowed by a heavy, numbing sense of desolation. His achievements mean little to him, his relationships are shallow and unsatisfying, and his nights are dominated by nightmares that are cinematic in their ability to replay the most harrowing aspects of his abuse. Despite the fact that his HIV is asymptomatic and it is likely his status will not reduce his lifespan, he relates it as if this were the 1980s, when a diagnosis was a form of death sentence.

The work with Jamie has a sluggish, dense quality, with all exchanges between us feeling as if they are being conducted in slow motion. He begins the session with a recap of how he has been feeling since our last session—usually tired, sad, or anxious. I respond, wondering what sparked these feelings, how they impacted on him, what connections he is able to make between his feelings and memories. He continues to look down at the carpet and a long silence develops, a silence I have become terribly familiar with. It is a silence that carries a dead weight, a silence that seems to obliterate thought and creativity in me. With other silent patients I seem far more able to remain alert and alive in the absence of words. At times the silence can feel creatively intimate, a shared space of reverie in which two separate unconsciouses are communicating. In Jamie's silence I can feel nothing that is terribly alive. Instead, I drift off, out of the room, finding myself daydreaming about anything other than Jamie, for when I do think about him I realise how easy it would be for me to sleep. Instead of engaging in the unconscious, I find myself at the edge of becoming unconscious.

I have to work hard with Jamie to recover myself, to pull myself back into the consulting room and fend off these deadening countertransference responses that threaten to sever any therapeutic connection between the two of us. Now that I have registered his lack of eye contact, it is clear that Jamie is working hard to address it, occasionally lifting his gaze to mine. It is obviously a tremendous burden for him, this most ordinary but most agonising of attainments. I am struck not by the colour of his eyes but by their deadness. In looking into his eyes I am reminded of the hollow, fathomless eyes of babies glimpsed over the years in television reports of famine in Sudan, Ethiopia and Somalia, their gazes blurred by the most primitive and annihilatory of traumas. I realise that these are not eyes I wish to look at for too long, so potent is the danger of being colonised by his sense of utter desolation and defeat. I alert myself to the risk of turning away my eyes from his, of Jamie experiencing my fear of the deadness he carries within him.

He attends every session, is never late and times his breaks to coincide with my own. This should gratify me, both narcissistically and as an indicator of his ability to use the therapy well. Instead I feel somewhat persecuted by his attendance, like a mother with a hungry baby who has come to think of herself as depleted, with nothing nourishing to give. I wonder whether he is ready to lie down on the couch, but reject the thought, fearing that such a move would sever any potential connection between us both. Our eyes would never then meet and I would never learn, as I think I have to, to bear the deadness of his gaze, and to develop ways of enlivening the gaze that meets his.

At times Jamie talks about suicide. He has made some attempts on his life but there has always been a passivity to these attempts, as if his depression chips away at itself, negating the agency he needs in order to make any kind of a mark on the world, even the most terrible mark of suicide. He berates himself for these failed attempts, providing as they do to him yet more evidence of his worthlessness—he cannot even kill himself properly.

I sometimes feel perversely twinned with Jamie, as if we are enmeshed through a sense of failure. I feel like a worthless therapist, with all my interpretations, my attempts to stir something alive in him, my efforts to contain and help process his trauma, all coming to nothing. I look to my supervision to provide some kind of life support system to this agonising lifeless work, but even find myself despairing of this, fearing that nothing can help dilute the despair that pervades our work. There are occasional glimpses of hope: an interpretation received and understood, or a relationship pursued in the external world. But never enough to relieve me of the fear that psychotherapy is, at best, a kind of sticking plaster, providing some form of structure to Jamie's world but doing so little to help him process the trauma he has experienced. I carry on with him, and know that he will probably continue with his therapy for years without either of us feeling that a corner has been turned, or his life has been transformed. I know that I feel terribly guilty about this. It is an awful thing to be faced with a patient who is more attached to despair than to hope. The attachment provides Jamie with a sense of self, albeit a perverse, desolate, and funereal one.

* * *

All psychotherapists and counsellors are familiar with what Christopher Bollas describes as "that familiar sinking feeling" (1989, p. 179) whenever a patient begins to tell their story of having been abused. Kluft describes those feelings of "bewilderment, exasperation and a sense of being drained" (1984a, p. 51) that accompany the hearing of a story of sexual trauma. These feelings are hugely magnified when the patient presents with the degree of deep, unmoving depression that Jamie brings with him. Depression and abuse are inextricably linked. It may be fended off through manic defences, or displaced into a variety of somatic, bipolar, or perverse symptoms, but it tends to run like a thread through the fabric of a male survivor's psyche. Childhood sexual abuse is associated with an increased risk of depression (Bifulco et al., 1991; Hanson et al., 2003; Widom et al., 2007). Fergusson and Woodward (2002) reported that a history of childhood sexual abuse increased the risk of depression by approximately four times. It is also a significant antecedent of suicidal behaviour (Bebbington et al., 2009), with childhood physical and violent sexual abuse representing the greatest risk factors for future suicide attempts (Joiner et al., 2007). Girls who have been sexually abused have a threefold increased risk of suicidal thoughts and plans, compared to non-abused girls. Boys who have been sexually abused have a ten-fold increased risk for suicidal plans and threats, and a fifteen-fold increased risk for suicide attempts, compared to non-abused boys.

Transgenerational abuse

I consider Jamie to be a victim of transgenerational abuse. It is unlikely that his parents were the first in his family to have broken the incest taboo. The process of the unconscious transmission of trauma between generations is found especially in families where there is an inhibition against thinking (Gardner, 1999). Maternal trauma of childhood sexual abuse has been identified as a risk factor for intergenerational abuse (Leifer et al., 2004b), with the risk being estimated at thirty per cent (Paredes et al., 2001). Belsky's (1993) ecological theory suggests that child abuse is determined by factors in the parent's history and personality, and by environmental, familial, and social factors that support or create stress for the parent. Attachment theory suggests it is the working models of the self, others, and self/other relationships that are transmitted across generations and account for continuity in abuse (Leifer et al., 2004a). Brothers (2014) suggests that one method of transmission from one generation to the next is through traumatic attachments. These attachments form within systems that, at some point in their histories, have been plunged into chaos by trauma. Once established, they tend to coalesce into patterns of relating so inflexible and resistant to change that they profoundly affect parent–child interactions over generations.

Hopeless patients

Freud's (1917e) seminal work *Mourning and Melancholia* differentiates the state of melancholia and the natural state of mourning, and uses this comparison to explore the psychic mechanisms of depression. This work has been followed by a rich parade of clinicians exploring both the psychogenesis of depression and the possibilities of treatment (Klein, 1940, reprinted 1975; Spitz & Wolf, 1946; Rado, 1951; Jacobson, 1954; Joffe & Sandler, 1964; Mendelson, 1974; Kohut, 1977; Bowlby, 1980; Bifulco et al., 1991; Steiner, 2005; Verhaeghe, 2008; Leader, 2009). It is clear that in treating patients such as Jamie we have a responsibility to measure the scale of the mountain we are seeking to climb.

Working with Jamie was, at times, like being in a stale marriage. We were both committed to the relationship (Jamie, perhaps, more than me) but could never ignore the hopelessness that permeated so many of our exchanges. I found myself questioning (not, it must be said, for the first time) whether there are victims who never become survivors. Are there men for whom the earliness of the abuse, the violence that accompanied it, and the close proximity of their abuser combine to shatter the potential for full psychic recovery? I think the most I could do for Jamie was to provide him with a safe space to which he could bring his despair. I presume he experienced some relief through this process, even if the relief was buried under the agonising weight of his daily miseries. The process of attending regular sessions, being listened to, and being in the presence of a benign, caring other may have done much to ward off the more worrying of his suicidal thoughts, giving him something of a reason to not destroy himself. How much the therapy enabled him to process the many impediments to contentment, if not happiness, I am less sure.

Beyond supportive psychotherapy

This is not to diminish the importance of the therapy. It is to contextualise it as something different from (but not necessarily less than) a psychodynamic process that, through the process of unconscious symptomology being made conscious through interpretation, leads to a processing of trauma. It is hard, of course, to know whether the therapy was staving off feelings of suicidal despair to the point where it was keeping Jamie alive. I think (and feel) there were times when it was. A key question concerns what, then, this form of psychotherapy with despairing and suicidal survivors actually is. It could be termed "supportive psychotherapy", although I think it important to avoid such a term diminishing the technical challenges of such work. In their paper "Beyond 'handholding': Supportive therapy for patients with BPD and self-injurious behavior" Hellerstein et al. highlight the ways in which supportive therapy has become synonymous with nonspecific treatment, with "just being nice to patients" (2004, p. 1). They outline the rigour with which this approach has been developed from perspectives as seemingly diverse as psychoanalytic (Kernberg, 1993) person-centred (Pinsker, 2014), and cognitive behavioural (Linehan, 1993) modalities, while also noting some key elements that demarcate it as its own unique form of treatment. They stress the need, for example, to avoid prolonged silent listening, neutrality, confrontation of resistance, or transference interpretations.

I came to learn with Jamie that his ego strength was too minimal for him to withstand these forms of interaction. His capacity for symbol formation was weak, with many forms of interpretation being experienced by him as aggressive attacks. He was easily wounded by my attempts to challenge his perception of the world as murderously threatening, devoid of joy or meaning. It was not *as if* the world was threatening. The sadistic and perverse elements of his parents' abuse of him had left him unable to hold in mind the metaphoric world of the phrase "as if". The world *was* threatening. Transference interpretation was particularly difficult for him to withstand, as his early experiences of trauma had blunted his capacity to differentiate between others as symbolic representations of early objects. With a less disturbed patient I would have been able to interpret his frustration at, for example, my imminent holiday, as being linked unconsciously with his loss of a good enough parental figure and the absence of safe attachment figures both in his childhood and his adult life. Jamie had to remain in the realm of the concrete—anything more symbolic was too intimidating for him to process. He was able to feel and express the loss of me over the break. He was not able to connect it with what it represented because this would have involved him connecting with emotions to do with his parents. He lacked what Bick (1968) called the "psychic skin" with which to think about his parents without a primitive fear that their abuse would resume.

It took me some time to realise and appreciate the fragility of Jamie's object relations and the impact this had on my capacity to be the kind of psychotherapist I was accustomed to being with my less ill patients. It should be said that the greatest learning I had in adapting my psychotherapeutic stance came not from my original psychoanalytic training but from the practice of many of my supervisees. I have the privilege of supervising the psychotherapists and counsellors at Survivors UK, the country's leading provider of individual and group therapy for male survivors of sexual abuse. The team is an eclectic one, coming from a broad range of trainings and orientations. What unites the clinicians there is a deep understanding of the sexual trauma of men and an abiding belief in relational therapy, regardless of theoretical orientation. I found myself soaking up many of their approaches in my work with Jamie, particularly those of the more creative clinicians whose work with highly disturbed patients over the years had equipped them to hold and contain many different versions of him.

I learned, as I have had to in my work with patients with intellectual disabilities (Corbett, 2009, 2011, 2014) that much of our original clinical trainings do not in fact prepare us to work with those whose experiences of severe and cumulative trauma have placed them at the very margins of human experience. The longer I have worked in the fields of trauma, abuse, disability, and dissociation, the more I have come to realise that too purist or singular a view of psychotherapy can only work with a relatively narrow band of patients. While I continue to think of myself and my work as decidedly psychoanalytic in framework, I have not been afraid of making use of other psychotherapeutic processes to reach those who, like Jamie, have found their connection to symbolic thinking fenced off by severe trauma.

A great deal of my work with Jamie used techniques such as:

- clarification—pointing out when a dysfunctional behavioural pattern was being repeated (a more direct, less interpretative way of understanding repetition compulsion);
- psychoeducation—providing guidance on symptoms of trauma that confused and frightened him;
- de-intensification—providing relief from the grip of emptiness, terror, and suicidal ideation.

Instead of going to the heat of the transference, interpreting unconscious enactments as they were being lived out between Jamie and I, I tended instead to "strike while the iron was cold" (Pine, 1984), waiting until the unbearable terror of the moment had passed, arriving at a moment of calm to look back safely at elements of our relationship he was in danger of feeling overwhelmed by.

Addiction to near death

At no time in my work with Jamie did my approach feel like "merely" supportive psychotherapy, twinned as it was with a psychoanalytic understanding of his deep attachment to despair. Betty Joseph introduced the concept of "addiction to near death" (Joseph, 1982) to describe a form of masochistic pathology she had observed in working with disturbed adolescents. Joseph came to understand her patients' wishes to gain a perverse, masochistic form of pleasure in attempts to destroy the self and the therapeutic relationship. She described this destruction as evoking libidinal satisfaction, despite its concomitant pain (an "awful pleasure"), evoking an addictive edge that can become immensely difficult to dislodge:

> There is a very malignant type of self-destructiveness, which we see in a small group of our patients, and which is, I think, in the *nature* of an addiction—an addiction to near-death. It dominates these patients' lives; for long periods it dominates the way they bring material to the analysis and the type of relationship they establish with the analyst; it dominates their internal relationships, their so-called thinking, and the way they communicate with themselves. It is not a drive towards a Nirvana type of peace or relief from problems, and it has to be sharply differentiated from this. The picture that these patients present is, I am sure, a familiar one—in their external lives these patients get more and more absorbed into hopelessness and involved in activities that seem destined to destroy them physically as well as mentally. (ibid., p. 449)

Joseph alerts us to the perverse pull towards desolation that overtakes the patient and threatens to submerge the therapy: "It seems to be like a constant pull towards despair and near-death, so that the patient is fascinated and unconsciously excited by the whole process … It is clearly extremely difficult for such patients to move towards more real and object-related enjoyments, which would mean giving up the all-consuming addictive gratifications" (p. 456). This places a useful slant on Jamie's despair, indicating counterintuitively that the agonies he brings to me provide him with a powerful secondary gain. The severity of his traumata and the paper-thinness of his psychic skin combine to make this aspect of his psyche tremendously difficult to interpret. His concretised defences would translate even the most tentative interpretation into an aggressive, murderous attack. We tread carefully with patients as ill as Jamie, and have to work hard to manage the complex countertransference responses that his addiction to anguish evokes. There were many times when I found myself harbouring feelings of murderous rage towards him, pushed, as I felt I was, to the edge of thought by his allegiance to desolation. His adhesive attachment to suicidality, self-hatred, and unmovable grief came to feel like a challenge to the hope I wished to embody to him. The higher he built his wall of hopelessness, the more shut out and, inevitably, angry, I became.

Counterresistances

Glover and Brierley's (1940) concept of the therapist's counterresistance is a useful one in considering the ways in which some of our more affective responses to our patients can be counterproductive. Chu discusses how "Patients in therapy may activate thoughts, feelings and fantasies in their therapists which their therapists attempt to fend off. Thus therapists' counterresistances, particularly in trying to cope with angry reactions or sadistic fantasies towards patients, can lead to therapists using such defences as reaction formation, avoidance or withdrawal" (2008, p. 212). Chu quotes Strean's explication of counterresistance as involving "over solicitousness; unnecessary reassurances; … postponing confrontations, questions or interpretations regarding a client's tardiness or absence, glossing over … the negative transference; and denying the existence of pathology, conflict or resistance in the client" (2014, p. 85).

I had to be aware that Jamie needed to evoke in me something akin to what Winnicott called hate in the countertransference (Winnicott, 1949). In order for us to reach the eventual aim of the therapy—Jamie's introjection of a good object through the movement from the paranoid/schizoid to the depressive position—it was not enough for me to attune only to the benign, positive, good-enough aspects of his psyche; I had to be aware of and open to the rage and hatred residing in him, the powerful residues of the incestuous triangle into which he had been born. At times my hatred of Jamie provided an invaluable insight into what it was like to live under an omnipresent cloud of self-loathing, what it felt like to be an object devoid of real, reciprocal love. By withstanding the waves of hatred that seemed to lie at the very essence of Jamie's DNA, I was providing an important buttress to him, a model of a good object which, over time, he could begin, slowly and incrementally, to introject.

Levels of interpretation

Much of the work with patients such as Jamie, whose primal experiences of trauma render them unable to use traditional notions of psychoanalytical psychotherapy, requires us to tune into what Alvarez called the right analytic wavelength (2012). She has formulated a level of interpretation that seeks to vitalise the deadened state of mind. This stands apart from the two other levels she has identified as being explanatory/locating or descriptive/naming interpretations, levels of interpretation that fit more neatly into a classic notion of analytic neutrality. What Alvarez is describing is a form of interpretation that recognises the need for something more enlivening, something that acknowledges the atrophied and deadened aspects of a patient's psyche, and that seeks not only to wake these parts up, but which also reminds the patient that the analyst has not been deadened by the patient's trauma. This was particularly pertinent when faced with Jamie's state of torment about his HIV status.

HIV and its impact

Rates of sexual abuse amongst people who are living with HIV/AIDS are significantly higher than for the general population (Batten et al., 2002; Kalichman et al., 2002; Leserman, 2005; Gwandure, 2007). Some survivors contracted HIV during the course of their abuse, while others' self-esteem has been so eroded by their abuse that they continue to place themselves in situations of high vulnerability to infection. As well as reporting greater anxiety, depression, suicidal ideation, and symptoms of borderline personality, survivors are significantly more likely to have had unprotected intercourse than those who have not been sexually assaulted. Prevailing norms of masculinity that expect men to be more knowledgeable and experienced about sex, put men, particularly young men, at risk of infection, because such norms prevent them from seeking information or admitting their lack of knowledge about sex or protection, and coerce them into experimenting with sex in unsafe ways, and at a young age, to prove their manhood (Gupta, 2000).

Psychotherapy with survivors who are HIV-positive adds another layer of trauma into the therapeutic matrix—a layer that can challenge the therapist to engage with intricate issues of illness and mortality (Cole, 2001). Samuels et al. (2011) discuss the role that childhood trauma plays in the resistance to engaging in psychotherapy exhibited by patients with AIDS. We have entered the "protease era" in which the meanings associated with HIV/AIDS can be considered in a different context: that of life continuing rather than inevitable or impending death. And yet for many male survivors (among others) the condition continues to carry the weight of associations with death, perverse sexuality, and decay. Much like the experience of having been sexually abused, an HIV/AIDS status can be a signifier of shame, a condition that evokes unconscious terrors of contamination and infection. The experience of living with HIV/AIDS cannot be separated from the social construction of HIV/AIDS as a stigmatised disease (Sontag, 1989; Petersen & Benishek, 2001) that carries projections of society's anxieties about illness and contagion (Joffe, 1999).

The stigma of infection

For Jamie, his HIV status was a stigma that seemed to him to be enmeshed with his status as a victim of incest. It had a different quality, however, being something that sparked immense fears about others being able to see that he was ill. This was a dangerous fantasy for him. In fact he rarely looked physically unwell, but seemed, through a dysmorphic process, to often see himself as underweight, haunted-looking, and ravaged by sickness. The word "stigma" carries a sense of physicality, referring as it originally did to a tattoo mark branded on the skin of an individual as a result of some incriminating action, identifying the person as someone to be avoided. From the 1600s it came to mean "a mark of disgrace", a visible emblem of those sins and disgraces that might otherwise have remained invisible. For those who become suicidal when they first receive their HIV diagnosis, suicidal thoughts are often rooted in the fear of isolation and discrimination that will come as a result of others finding out about the disease, rather than as a result of the disease itself (Carr, 2002).

Jamie often described his diagnosis as carrying with it an inevitability that stemmed from his experiences of childhood abuse. All roads seemed, in his mind, to have led to this condition he equated with disease and, ultimately, death. Small wonder that the weight of his diagnosis on top of the impact of a childhood saturated by perversity and abuse resulted in a presentation of almost catatonic depression. Withstanding the pain of a life lived in the shadow of abuse and illness exerted a terrible price upon Jamie's capacity to find anything joyful or life-affirming in his existence. There were times when he needed me to identify wholly with his despair, when I too had to be subject to the suffocating claustrophobia of his anguish, to the point where I found myself wondering about the worth of our work. There were other times when it was more important for me to identify with the pleasure principle than the death instinct (Freud, 1920g).

It was at these moments that I made use of Alvarez's (2012) notion of the enlivening interpretative stance, in an attempt to connect with those slithers of dynamism that occasionally emerged through the cracks of Jamie's melancholy. A moment of eye contact or the reporting of a hopeful conversation with a friend had to be amplified by me, otherwise they tended to be consumed and erased by the force of his depression. I had to, at times, take on the role of auxiliary ego, holding in mind those moments of hope that would otherwise have evaporated within the hothouse of his harsh superego. While taking seriously the enormity of his medical condition—bearing in mind the need for work with patients who test positive for HIV/AIDS to involve a sensitive, careful, and thorough biopsychosocial assessment with specific, detailed attention to the impact of the diagnosis (Rubenstein & Sorrentino, 2007)—I had to be careful to avoid an over-identification with those aspects of his condition that touched on his sense of himself as someone who did not deserve to live. The work with Jamie was often exhausting, so intricately did I have to navigate my way through the cracks of his fragile ego.

The capacity for hope

One of the questions I am posing in this chapter is whether there are men who never recover from the trauma of sexual abuse. It is a difficult question to answer. There are men whose experiences of trauma have removed from them much capacity for spontaneity, joy, and security, but for whom therapy can provide an essential sense of holding and containment. The power and impact of this should not be underestimated. For these men psychotherapy has to adopt a different shape, rhythm, or set of aims from psychotherapy with healthier patients. Recovery from trauma involves a process of mourning. For the male survivor this includes the mourning of loss of childhood, the removal of psychic and bodily integrity, and a catastrophic assault upon masculinity. Zetzel (1970) makes the ability to mourn a criterion for psychoanalytic treatment. I suggest that the ability to mourn depends largely on the capacity for hope. It is the absence of hope that loss can be survived that kills off the energy required to process major trauma. Schachtel (1959) distinguished two forms of hope. One is compared to Pandora's Box, the patient coming to his sessions with utter passivity, close to despair. He has limited resources with which to open the box containing his traumata. Any hope of the lid being lifted lies in the therapist. The patient himself has no power. A second type of hope stems from a person's capacity to actualise his life, a more hopeful view of the potential potency of the patient who is able to make use of his own reserves in the service of the therapy. The therapist is not expected to do all the heavy lifting.

The work of regeneration

Alvarez has "looked for a word or concept (for) the birth and development of hope in a child who may have been clinically depressed all his life. The nearest I can get is … the 'work of regeneration' or, to paraphrase Daniel Stern and George Herbert, the 'slow momentous discovery that his shrivelled heart can contain greenness'" (1992, p. 173). In discussing the treatment of a patient who held little or no hope that therapy could help him, Ogden said "he did not have to like therapy or feel that it could help him. He just had to be there" (1982, p. 123). Through this statement, Ogden is reinforcing the notion that there are times with hopeless patients when the therapist has to act as a container for hopeful feelings that do not exist within the patient, and there are times when we have to make this conscious for our patients. The fact that they feel depleted of all hope of effecting change does not mean hope cannot reside in another. The fact of one part of a dyad feeling dead does not have to kill off the other part of the dyad.

This is the type of patient that McDougall (1992) calls the "anti-analysand", whose resistance to finding meaning threatens to disable the therapist's main rejoinder to hopelessness—that is to say, the therapist's own hope. Once this has gone, how possible is it to carry on? A vital quality of depressive despair is "the sense of being trapped in a way of living that is anguishing and can't be changed" (Bonime, 1982, p. 174). It is vital, diagnostically, to be able to recognise this aspect of a survivor's pathology in the place where it tends to resonate most strongly: our countertransference. When we feel as if we are entrapped by the despair of our patient, we need to consider both what the aetiology and the function of such despair is. I suggest there can be an aggressive component to the level of almost catatonic depression that patients such as Jamie present. It renders us impotent to resist its pull, echoing the powerlessness felt by the patient at the hands of his abuser. It destroys the capacity to think and removes from us access to creativity. Without creativity the consulting room becomes a sterile and barren place. The spontaneous, playful turn-taking of therapist–patient exchanges is suffocated by the weight of despair and, if we allow our minds to mirror the mindlessness of our patient, therapy loses its mutative potential.

The deeply depressed and despairing patient issues us with a challenge to survive. His hopelessness becomes a perverse re-enactment of abuse, in which he passively assumes the role of silent, oppressive abuser and we become the broken-down, muted child. We thus need to demonstrate our resilience through survival. At times this will necessitate the use of Alvarez's enlivening levels of interpretation, affect-filled interventions that promote liveliness in both us and our patient. At other times this will require simply remaining in our chair, keeping our eyes open, and staying alive. The cumulative power of aliveness in the face of deadening depression should not be underestimated. Over time the patient will introject the continuing survival of the therapist, gradually letting in those nano-bytes of aliveness that have previously served to illustrate the difference between the deadened patient and the enlivened world.

CHAPTER SIX

Dying to be a woman: grievances and attacks on gender

I have been expecting "Simon", but find myself facing "Simone". Simon's therapy has been characterised since its beginning by constant manic change. There have been weeks when he has sought to convince me that the answer to his pain was to marry a woman, to disavow the homosexual thoughts and fantasies that he was terrified of enacting. There were other weeks when he described himself as now being totally asexual, finding relief in abstinence not just from action, but from thought and desire. Lately he has sought refuge in a new idea: that he can avoid the vicissitudes of homo- or heterosexuality by becoming a transsexual, an inter-gendered being occupying a liminal place on the gender divide. Each new idea is entered into with frenzied determination, the paranoid/schizoid aspects of Simon becoming galvanised in the service of a manic defence against the realities of his history of abuse.

For some sessions Simon has been experimenting with displaying the more feminine aspects of his personality (having blusher on his face or wearing a woman's scarf), but today is the first time he has dared to show me what he looks like when he dresses as a woman. He is clearly nervous and, as usual when he finds himself overwhelmed by anxiety, overlays his fears with a facade of aggression. "You're to call me Simone—that's my name," he tells me, the feminine lilt to his voice laden with a harsh edge of anger. "Simon's not here today. I don't know if you'll see him again," he continues. "I want to talk about the future. The past is in the past. It's gone. You look a little shocked—are you? You shouldn't be—you know lately I've been dying to be a woman."

I realise that I am, in fact, deeply shocked by Simon's appearance. I had supposed that one day he would summon up the courage to show me this aspect of himself, but I had imagined there would be some warning. It is clear he wants me to be shocked, partly as a way of relieving the immense feelings of powerlessness he has struggled with throughout the year we have been seeing each other. I put it to him that he has enacted something tremendously powerful by dressing as a woman without any prior notice, and I wonder what this has done to his more familiar feelings of fear and impotence. He berates me for my question, saying that I have not been listening to him—I am relating to him as if he were still Simon when today he is Simone, a new creation. The past has been cleaved off, today is all that matters. I realise I have been backed into a corner. It is hard to know how gently non-questioning I should be about Simon's appearance, as opposed to how challenging I should be about what he is acting out in front of me. The session continues with me struggling to know quite where to locate myself in relation to this new and unknown aspect of my patient. Simon himself appears thrilled by his actions, at least until ten minutes before the end of the session, when he begins to consider what it will be like to leave the consulting room to brave the ridicule and cruelty of the outside world. Without wanting to be caught in a split between Simon and Simone, I reflect that this sadness and anxiety feel more familiar and are, in fact, emblematic of the struggles Simon has in relating to the outside world. Simon cries for a while, acknowledging that the impressively confident performance he has just enacted brings with it a crucial question of identity for him: who should he be in the world?

The following session Simon returns, and reports having struggled with overwhelming feelings of sadness since we last saw each other. He had, he says, hoped that dressing as Simone would lance the feelings of pain he had been laden with throughout the course of his therapy, since he had started telling me his story of abuse. His childhood had been characterised by constant change and movement. Being the son of army parents, he tended to only stay in one home for a maximum of twelve months before being forced to uproot and move on. While stationed in Scotland at the age of ten he had befriended another child in the army camp, a girl five years older than him. Within a few weeks of meeting, their play had become highly sexualised, with the older girl eventually taking the lead in a series of "games" that tended to involve Simon masturbating and eventually performing oral sex on her. She swore him to secrecy and threatened violent retribution should the abuse ever be disclosed. True to his word, Simon told nobody about the abuse, repressing the feelings of shame and revulsion he had been left with, alongside other more troubling feelings of excitement and arousal.

Simon gradually recognised he was homosexual as he entered adolescence. The discovery was horrifying to him, fused as it was with associations with abuse. He feared that his homosexuality had been caused by his abuse, the actions of the older girl instilling in him a phobic response to the idea of heterosexual sex. For some years he repressed his sexuality, forcing himself to engage in abortive sexual relationships with girls, relationships in which he felt no arousal and no enjoyment. Eventually he seemed to come to terms with his sexuality, and "came out" to a small group of friends. His experiences of trying to meet men and pursue intimate relationships were catastrophic. He discovered that he was unable to sustain any level of sexual intimacy with another man, his attempts at closeness being obliterated by a set of paranoid reactions that rendered him impotent. He persevered for some time but eventually had to acknowledge defeat in the face of his traumatogenic responses to any form of sexual closeness. Since then he had sublimated his sexual drives into a range of other activities, occasionally engaging in bouts of masturbation to internet pornography, but more usually seeking to cut off any feelings of sexual desire, to reinvent himself as an asexual being.

The sessions following the introduction of Simone saw Simon beginning to articulate what was probably his greatest emotional challenge: a deeply embedded sense of identity confusion. His hopes that adopting the persona of Simone would provide him with some relief had ended in disappointment. The danger was that he would soon start to construct another false and manic solution to the enigma of his life. His experiences of abuse had not simply left him with questions around his sexual orientation or his gender identity, they had produced a state of existential bemusement, a perpetual state of unknowing. His manic attempts at identifying with an external sense of self were catastrophic, as they were false self (Winnicott, 1965) constructions. Ultimately, Simon's disastrous attempt to inhabit the skin of Simone resulted in him achieving a deeper level of engagement in his therapy, to the point where he was finally able to piece together the many terrible fragments of his narrative of abuse. Before, he had reported the abuse to me as if recounting the plot of a book he had read many years before. His account lacked affect and served to confuse me yet further as to how best to help him—a feeling of confusion that also had a powerful projective function. I was learning what it was like to be Simon, to not know, to stumble after answers, and to have to live with uncertainty.

For Simon the gender of his abuser mattered far more than the components of the abuse itself, rendering him immobile before a set of terrifying assumptions that the fact she was female had destroyed something fundamental about his sense of maleness. Eventually he was able to reclaim his sense of his homosexuality as being ego syntonic rather than a perverse ego dystonic response to trauma. The work with him required something of a psycho-educative component at times, so confused was he about the impact of female abuse upon his gender identity. Our work together continued to challenge the two of us, touching as it so often had to on this fault line running beneath his sense of identity, forcing him to confront his ongoing belief that being abused by a female meant he would forever be a pariah, an outsider in a world in which genders and sexualities were painfully hard to identify safely with.

* * *

We tend to think of our awareness of women as abusers as being a contemporary development, and yet it has been glimpsed throughout the history of literature, way back to the first century work of fiction *Satyricon*, where we see rapes orchestrated by the female Quartilla (Gill, 1973). Ambroise Tardieu included female perpetrators in his study of hundreds of cases of incest against children in the nineteenth century (Labbé, 2005) while Bender and Blau documented the case of a six-year-old boy who had been sexually abused by his mother—although the boy was identified as the guilty party, having made "sex advances with his mother" (1937, p. 502). Abuse by women tends to be minimised by social services, police, and the criminal justice system (Hayes & Carpenter, 2013). Clements, Dawson and das Nair (2014) found professionals working with offenders of both genders in the UK, Australia, and Canada believed that abuse perpetrated by a woman is more harmful than abuse perpetrated by a man.

Attitudes towards female sexual aggression

Some of these beliefs stem from a core problem in conceptualising women as being capable of sexual aggression, with men's aggression being understood as an extension of essentially masculine behaviour and women's aggression being impossible to place on a continuum of normative femininity. In her pioneering psychoanalytic study of female perpetrators, *Mother, Madonna, Whore,* Welldon (1988) contrasts society's idealisation of women as natural maternal caregivers who sexually offend only if they are incited to by a man with her clinical experience of women whose actions are as perverse, dangerous, and damaging as those of any male abuser. Her patients seem capable of acts of perversion that do not, on the whole, depend on the coercion or instruction of a male partner. The abuse of boys or men by women tends to be theorised as the result of something unplanned, unlike the actions of male abusers. While women are idealised, their capacity to abuse and, not only to abuse, but to abuse with perverse intent, seems unthinkable (Hetherton, 1999). As Mathis ironically states: "that she might seduce a child into sex play is unthinkable and even if she did so what harm could she do without a penis?" (1972, p. 53).

A collective societal denial about the incidence and aetiology of female sexual offending has tremendous implications not just in terms of the prioritisation of resources to work with this forensic population, but also for the boy or man whose abuser was female. If we at the very least misunderstand or at the worst actively deny that women can abuse for similar reasons and with as profound an emotional impact as men, we are at risk of denying or misunderstanding the needs of the victim it is our job to understand. Men who have been abused by women suffer from a conflation of societal denials—that men can be abused, and that women can abuse. Parsons (1954) claimed that mother–son abuse is invariably the most damaging form of incest. Margolin (1985) challenged this view, concluding from a review of cases that responses to this type of incest are multidimensional, representing an extraordinary range of behaviour not foreseen by Parsons. Margolin concluded that the effects of mother–son incest are related to the symbolic meanings attributed to this act by the participants. Denov's (2004) study into the experience and long-term impact of sexual abuse by women identified victims' long-term difficulties with substance abuse, self-injury, suicide, depression, rage, strained relationships with women, self-concept and identity issues, and a discomfort with sex.

Manic flights from gender

A key aim of my work with Simon was to relieve him of the pressure of concretised thinking. His solutions to the agony of childhood sexual abuse tended to involve manic flights from gender and sexuality, in his case from maleness and homosexuality. This is not an unusual phenomenon in work with male survivors, abuse often leaving a trail of deep confusion about gender and sexual identity (Gartner, 1999; Tremblay & Turcotte, 2005). It is important that the role of trauma is included in our thinking about the development of gender dysphoria (Zucker & Kuksis, 1990) and it was vital that I maintained a respectful position of curiosity about Simon's apparent wish to kill off a part of his psyche through his "dying to be a woman". While I doubted that he was one of those patients for whom a transgender identify stems from a deeply embodied, lifelong experience of one's gender occupying the wrong body (Eagly et al., 2004; Byne et al., 2012), it was essential I did not foreclose our mutual exploration of the aetiology of his gender confusion.

Unlike patients for whom maintaining the wrong gender in the wrong body represents a form of psychic annihilation, Simon's abandonment of his feminine identity appeared to relieve him, opening up a less concretised way of thinking about the function of his desire. This would not have been the case were he to fulfil the criteria of gender dysphoria (Harris, 2002; Lev, 2004). These distinctions are crucial to note as we come to treat more transgendered patients for whom the experience of sexual violation is the presenting symptom, rather than gender confusion. One in two of those who identify as transgender are sexually abused or assaulted at some point in their lives (Kenagy, 2005). Some reports estimate that transgender survivors may experience rates of sexual assault up to sixty-six per cent, often coupled with physical assaults or abuse (Bradford et al., 2013).

Simon's abuse represented a fundamental attack on his sense of self, rendering him vulnerable to a lifelong search for a new self that could obliterate the debilitating sense of hatred and loathing that assailed him every time he looked in the mirror. Winnicott's concept of self encompassed both Freudian notions of the ego and the id, underpinning the centrality of a resilient self with which to attain creative and fulfilling emotional well-being (Winnicott, 1960). Simon's confusion as to his sexuality and his gender may be understood as forms of false self functioning (Winnicott, 1965), dysfunctional responses to annihilatory anxiety that involve the building of defences with which the traumata of abuse can be held at bay. Whereas Winnicott tended to conceptualise false self functioning as a defence that complies with the expectations of others, I have come to think of it more as a traumatogenic barrier that serves to divert the gaze of the other away from that which the patient most fears. In Simon's case, what his various false selves attempted to conceal was the conglomeration of shame, horror, and self-hatred stemming from his experiences of being abused by a girl. Such was the scale of humiliation engendered by this that Simon could not bear to be himself; his self had to die to be replaced by another.

As we have seen, survivors of male abuse are vulnerable to anxieties about homosexuality, whatever their sexual orientation actually is. Simon struggled to comprehend that his sexuality was not formed by sexual trauma. It was undoubtedly compromised and complicated but not formed by trauma. I wish to contrast this case with that of a patient whose relationship with gender was far more concretely conflicted and whose inability to process both the trauma of abuse and his relationship with his core sense of gender made therapeutic processing an almost impossible task.

* * *

"Dave" handed me a letter of complaint. I immediately worried that the complaint was against me, a fear I suddenly recognised as having bothered me on a subliminal level since I had begun seeing Dave some months before. It was in fact a complaint about his keyworker, Gabriel. Dave had mild intellectual disabilities, and had been referred to the clinic where I worked following a disclosure of childhood sexual abuse. He had told a member of staff in the home in which he lived that he had been abused by his mother. His memories of the abuse were vague and he was unable to describe at which age it had started or finished. All he could say was that his mother, who was now long dead, was a bad woman who did bad things. Whenever the abuse actually happened, it had been when Dave was a girl. Two years before his referral to me he had embarked on gender reassignment, and now lived, mostly, as a woman. I say "mostly" because the process had been halted six months before, owing to health concerns raised by Dave's obesity. His weight had rocketed since beginning his hormone treatment, not helped by what seemed to be an insatiable hunger for fatty food. The non-surgical side of his transition continued, with surgery put on hold until his weight, and the reasons behind its increase, stabilised.

I ask Dave to explain to me what has caused him to make a complaint about Gabriel. His face reddens, and he begins to shout: "He's a bastard, a fucking bastard. He called me that name. That fucking name!" Dave shakes, and I can see he is building up to another of the panic attacks that have punctuated our work together. I encourage him to remember what has helped before—to breathe deeply, to regulate this anxiety that threatens to take him over. After a while he calms somewhat, and he tells me that Gabriel had used Dave's pre-treatment name ("Veronica") when waking him the previous day. "He said it just slipped out," he says, his voice electric with fury, "but I know it wasn't a fucking mistake. He wants to hurt me. He thinks he can hurt me. But he can't. No one can fucking hurt me now! But I'm gonna hurt him! I'm gonna make him suffer—make him get the sack. That's what's gonna happen to him!" I underscore Dave's fury, stating how terrible it is that he has been so hurt by Gabriel using that name he hates. It must, I venture, rather nervously, put him in touch with the body he hated, the one he wanted to get rid of. Unlike previous sessions, where any mention of his pre-male gender has provoked a tidal wave of anger, Dave hears my curiosity in the benign tone with which it is offered. "Yeah," he says, "I hate it. Hate thinking of her. Hated being her. Not good to be …" I see that, once again, he is stopping himself from using that most abhorred word in his vocabulary: "woman". "Not good to be—that. That thing. I'm tough now, ain't I? Don't need to worry about getting hurt. No one can hurt me now!"

Encouraged by a slight lowering of the aggressive defences that often impede a softer, more reciprocal exchange between us, I suggest to Dave that, actually, "it *is* possible for men to be hurt. Not only women have to deal with powerful feelings, and perhaps *you* can feel hurt, just as Veronica was." This is too much for Dave to bear. Dave experiences the name "Veronica", and the suggestion that he may share some of her vulnerabilities, as a narcissistic wound, and he says he has to stop the session. I am in danger of causing him to complain about me, my unconscious fear made conscious. I try to stop him from leaving the session, but it is clear that I have broken the unspoken code between us. I have dared to link him too concretely with this feminine self that he has disavowed and in doing so I have brought him too close to an agony that cannot be assuaged by changing gender.

* * *

Psychoanalytic attitudes towards gender change

The notion of changing gender tends to evoke anxiety, not least in the therapist faced with a patient who resists the invitation to think symbolically about the transition they wish to make. We may struggle to know where to place ourselves in relation to our patient. Is our primary function to question the patient's core assumptions that they have been born into the wrong body? Should we facilitate a less interrogative space in which the pain underlying the decision can be thought about and processed? Can we provide a neutral space of thought and reflection despite our own assumptions, prejudices and fears about the whole notion of a gender being transformed? In his account of his group analytic work with men with gender disorders Hakeem (2012) notes an evaluative shift in focus over time. Early work with gender confusion mirrored the narrow, binary experiences prevalent in many transgendered patients who felt that they had to be confined to one gender construct or switch to another. More recently, clinicians have conveyed a therapeutic attitude that is more accepting of uncertainty and ambiguity, rather than rigid adherence to both heterosexual and binary gender idealism (Wright, 2006; Hakeem, 2010).

Hakeem highlights the importance of promoting curiosity within the patient about their gender, avoiding too premature and concrete a definition of himself as transvestite, transsexual, or other. For some male survivors there is an understandable wish to obliterate a core identity that is experienced as a victim self. Maleness is reduced to a conflation of vulnerability and aggression, both aspects of the self that are too much to hold in mind safely. States of transgenderism or transsexualism may be clung onto by the survivor like a drowning man holding onto a life raft. Nothing is to be gained by the therapist mirroring this polarised stance. Empathic, respectful, and neutral curiosity must be modelled in order for a true analysis of the aetiology of gender confusion to be undertaken.

Such a position is difficult to attain and harder to sustain when faced with trauma of the magnitude suffered by Veronica and held by Dave. Dave eventually returned to our sessions, although it has to be said that the alliance between us tended to be a fragile one and he did eventually make a complaint against me. As with all of his complaints he had chosen a concrete and incredible instance of my negligence to convey his deeper sense of me as someone who had failed to collude with his fantasy that all the pain of abuse resided in Veronica, making the killing-off of her a killing-off of the legacy of trauma. It was hard not to see our work as a failure, and I think I was premature in my attempts to promote ways of thinking about the symbolic function of changing one gender for another.

The work with Dave was complicated by the fact that the abuse he suffered appears to have started in a pre-verbal stage. It was hard for him to put words to something that assailed him before he himself had words, thus making the forming of a narrative an elusive therapeutic goal for him to attain. Hatred towards his abuser had become redirected against himself, Veronica performing the role of hated object in the absence of her mother. An intricate fusion had taken place between Veronica as the aggressor and Veronica as the passive victim. Dave was clear that Veronica had to be killed off because she had allowed abuse to happen, and personified everything he assumed to have caused the crimes of his mother. To be female was to be weak, passive, collusive, and abusive. It is possible that if Dave's rage could have been more safely contained within the sessions he may have been able to continue his work and process the complexities of his relationship with his gender. Sadly, just as we can view his switch from female to male as an attack upon his abuser and himself, his attack upon me in the form of a complaint was another enactment of unprocessed rage.

Attacks upon the therapist

All psychotherapists working with anyone other than the mythological "worried well" are vulnerable to attack. There will be times when the failure to interpret correctly or at the right time can be experienced as a catastrophic wound by the patient whose response can be to attack with all the ferocity with which they feel they have been attacked. Dave's grievance against me was linked to his grievance against his body and, as we have seen, against his mother. His body had allowed itself to be attacked; it had shown a dreadful vulnerability that continued to cause Dave an agony that could rarely be ignored. All he could do at this point of the therapy was launch an attack upon me, hopeful that this would relieve him of the agony with which he lived. The complaint came at a moment where Dave did seem to be gaining more insight into the aetiology of his fury, a time of hope for us both. It is unsurprising, in hindsight, to note how overwhelmed he was by the notion of recovery.

To be complained about is one of the most unsettling fears held by psychotherapists. Our professional worlds are usually quite small, and our livelihoods tend to depend on our reputations. Even when complaints have been investigated and found to be unwarranted, the smoke from the imagined fire takes time to clear. There are, of course, fraudulent and corrupt practitioners who deserve to be reported and who should not be practising. In some ways these are the relatively easier cases to adjudicate, as it can be seen that the pathology resides in the therapist rather than the patient. The far more complex cases are those where complex transferential processes have resulted in the enactment of an aggressive attack upon the therapy. The fact that sexual abuse is an attack, an assault on the body as well as the mind, makes all of us working in this field particularly vulnerable to facing an attack upon the body of our work. The relationship between therapist and patient is such a profoundly complex and sensitive one that any perceived misattunement can be experienced by the patient as a further assault upon his very being. The word grievance has its roots in grief, and was originally used to describe the act of inflicting harm on another. A grievance can be an enactment of grief, a visceral way of transmitting the patient's profound losses into the therapist, robbing the practitioner of power and relieving the patient of his helplessness.

By the time a patient has lodged a formal complaint against the therapist, a rupture has occurred that tends to be irreparable. Formal complaints procedures are rarely sophisticated enough to sieve through the nuances of a false allegation, and struggle to differentiate between the real (where the therapist has, through negligence or malice, abused the patient in some way), the imaginary (where the patient's pathology has caused delusional thinking to prevail over reality), or the symbolic (where the patient has been slighted by the therapist's misattunement, badly timed interpretation or momentary lack of thinking).

The symbolic is the most difficult to adjudicate on, as it involves complex transferential processes that tend to be vividly experienced by the patient and the therapist, but are barely visible or audible to those outside the consulting room. These dynamics are heightened by the patient's previous experiences of being the subject of the most appalling abuses and, usually, of never having attained any sense of justice for these injuries. When the transference has become overly concretised it can be difficult for the patient to retain his capacity for "as if" functioning. It is no longer as if the therapist is his abusing father or his collusive mother. He is both.

Attacks upon gender

The impact of a man's abuser being female is lodged on many different levels of a patient's internal world. The depth of the wound is worsened by society's capacity to deny that women can do sexual harm to men, leaving the survivor struggling for any kind of validation of his experiences. The wound is particularly toxic if the abuser is the man's mother or grandmother—it is in these cases where we see the most extraordinarily painful and long-lasting disturbances to sense of self, sexuality, and gender. In working with survivors with confusion about their gender we need to be cautious as to the function of their curiosity. As can be seen in the contrast between Simon and Dave, there are profound differences between the man who feels he has been born into the wrong body and the man whose core sense of masculinity has been compromised by sexual abuse. Those cases where both states exist are the most complex of all.

I have chosen to examine the impact of sexual abuse upon gender identity alongside the impact of complaints against the therapist as both phenomena concern a core grievance that begins as symbolic and, unless managed carefully and sensitively, threatens to move too quickly to the concrete. While there are those for whom the gender they have been born with is not the gender they can live with, there are others for whom gender identity relates more strongly to a disturbance wrought by sexual trauma. While our job is not to adjudicate for or against the choices made by our patients, it is our responsibility to help promote thinking about the possible connections between sexual abuse and the wish to disavow the gender with which one has been born. Simon personifies a deeply gendered confusion that is connected to traumatogenic processes. This applies to Dave as well, while his case is a more complex one given his level of intellectual disability and the much more highly defended resistance he has to examining the possibility that gender and abuse are linked.

The enactment of hatred

What both men had in common is the enactment of hatred. They were both in thrall to a persecutory object relationship that had shredded their sense of self, leaving them in a profound state of existential confusion. Most patients come to the consulting room asking, in a variety of ways, "Who am I?" Simon and Dave were also asking, "What am I?", their experiences of trauma touching not only on their capacity to retain a sense of self but also on their capacity to identify clearly with one gender over another. Such cases are rarely amenable to a simplistic formulation by which gender confusion can be ascribed to early object-relational failures, later sexual trauma, or a much earlier congenital condition. Each attack on the self is enough on its own to produce heightened states of confusion and despair as to the nature of one's gendered self. The combination of all three is a more profound catastrophe that requires the most delicate therapeutic interventions. Small wonder that such therapy tends to be practised on tremendously thin ice, with the patient at risk of perceiving his therapist as being the personification of society's ambivalence and bewilderment about gender change. This work is vulnerable to a form of projective identification by which the slightest mis-attunement between therapist and patient can result in the patient feeling judged, stigmatised, and ultimately failed by his therapist. For some patients the only option is to withdraw, to abandon their treatment before the pain increases. For others, the attack felt by the patient has to be evacuated into the therapist—the grief must be concretised into a grievance.

To avoid the pitfalls of this delicate area of work requires a certain elasticity of attitude regarding gender, and not just in how we respond to the patient whose gender is causing them profound agony. We also need to be attuned to the particularly toxic pain left behind by the sting of female abuse. Too concrete an attitude towards gender results in too polarised a split between men as abusers and women as victims. Women are perpetrators too and this may induce in the male survivor a profound and debilitating confusion about his own gender identity.

Most female abuse is incestuous, adding a further injury to the boy's sense of self. Once the incest taboo has been broken it can be difficult to live without a perpetual fear of all boundaries being permeable. Where sexual abuse has been enacted, it is vital that the survivor's desire to alter gender is viewed through the lens of trauma. We need to attend to the possibility that the wish to transition from one gender to another stems from an unconscious desire to kill off both the victim and the perpetrator.

CHAPTER SEVEN

Starving for two: working with embodied trauma

"Frazer" was a victim of drug rape. A hopeful first date had ended with Frazer waking alone in a hotel room, his body bruised, his anus bleeding. He recalled the beginning of the evening, meeting his date in a bar following a series of email exchanges. They had first made contact via a mobile phone app, and Frazer remembered feeling relieved that this man, George, was attractive, chatty, and easy company. As the night progressed, however, it became clear to Frazer that there was little sexual chemistry between them, and he talked about having to leave to prepare for an early morning work meeting. George insisted on Frazer having one more drink, which he agreed to, reluctantly. After this his memories grew hazy and indistinct. Initially he recalled snippets of what had transpired, micro-flashbacks of feeling dizzy following the last drink, a cab journey in the dead of night, and vague recollections of being in the hotel room in which he later woke. Over the course of the next few days Frazer's memories increased, and he recalled being subject to a sadistic, physically violent rape. The component parts of the rape began to fit together like pieces of a jigsaw puzzle, although some parts remained missing, and perhaps always will.

Fearing a humiliating and sceptical response from the police, Jamie never reported the rape, and told none of his friends about it, beyond alluding to a sexual encounter that had been rougher than he would have liked. He experienced regular flashbacks to the rape, his sleep being punctuated by horrific nightmares, his body continuing to hold an ongoing sense of intrusion and penetration. He cut himself off from many of his friends, and never dared to go out on a date again. Apart from this, the most visible legacy of his rape lay in Frazer's body shape. Before, he had been fairly plump, not grossly overweight, but clearly someone who did not care too much about what he ate. Without quite realising how and when it began, he embarked on a series of diets, transforming his body in quite dramatic ways. Alongside this he began to attend the gym obsessively, to the point where it became at least a daily ritual. Within a year of his attack Jamie was unrecognisable, his life revolving around the foods he could and could not eat and his daily sessions at the gym. By the time he entered therapy it was clear that his obsession with what could enter his body had assumed pathological proportions. He had to work extremely hard to maintain and develop his increasingly muscled body while also monitoring to an obsessive degree the calories he consumed.

By the time I met him Frazer's life was shaped around his body. He was a freelance consultant in the arms sector, and had cut back on the amount of contracts he took on in order to allow him enough time to visit the gym a minimum of twice a day. His obsession with food had progressed to the feverish state of an eating disorder, with every morsel of food he consumed being subject to detailed analysis and evaluation. Most of his friends had left him, unable to relate anymore to this obsessive, narcissistic man whose personality appeared to have altered as much as his body shape. As he described the relatively normal, if slightly overweight, body shape he had had before the attack, it was difficult to equate this with the lean, toned, and hugely muscular figure he now presented.

In attempting to think with Frazer about the extent to which food and exercise seemed to be regulating his life, it became clear that what he saw when he looked in the mirror was markedly different from what was seen by others. He described himself as a "work in progress", someone whose body required months, perhaps years, more work until it could be said to have reached a satisfactory shape. His descriptions of what he saw when he looked in the mirror did not match what I saw before me. "I'm still pudgy," he explained. "I need to work hard to get rid of that. I'd like to be toned—get rid of this fat." I realised that what he saw in his mirror was a reflection of himself at the time of his rape. His musculature was invisible to him, his body representing ugliness, fragility, weakness, and an awful vulnerability. Just as there was a stiffness about Frazer's body, his muscles being so pumped up it was hard for him to move with much ease or dexterity, it became clear that his mind was similarly encumbered. There was a slowness to his thoughts, his ability to take in interpretations was terribly limited, to the point where I came to see my words as being like bits of food he dared not swallow. Just as food represented the intrusive, danger-laden abuser, there was a risk that he would have to place me within the same negative transference. He was, I realised, caught in the immediate aftermath of his abuse, his mind and body frozen in a state of perpetual hypervigilance. He was like a solider away from the front, unable to feel the safety of home, constantly mistaking everyday sounds for the clamour and terror of war. His body was a flak jacket, designed to protect him from enemy fire but too unwieldy to allow him to move with any ease or comfort through daily life. His mind was similarly encased in protective shielding, forcing him to constantly view the outside world through a lens of distrust, panic, and fear.

The first year of our work together involved the slow building of a therapeutic alliance in which Frazer could experience me as a brother in arms rather than an enemy warrior. I was a recruit he had to train in the codes of conduct of his war. I had to be equipped to understand the seeming impossibility of him giving up his daily manoeuvres, and to comprehend the military precision with which he allowed food in and out of his body. Nothing about his war could be questioned until I was firmly embedded on his side. Once this had been achieved it became possible to gently work away at the reasons why war had been declared, allowing him to hear interpretations without experiencing them as an enemy attack. Over time he allowed himself to be interested in my curiosity about what had provoked the war—the rape itself. I had to tread carefully: the transference was still rooted in a fragile, tentative alliance and I was aware of how quickly and easily I could be banished behind enemy lines. Eventually it became possible to talk about a possible peace, the idea of living a normal life "in civvies", divested of the stifling weight of his defences. It was slow, sometimes agonising, work, as understanding the reasons for the totalitarian grip over him of diet and exercise involved returning to the annihilatory terror of the night he was raped—an experience made more difficult to process because so much of it had been obliterated by whatever drug his rapist had used on him.

* * *

The somatisation of trauma

Frazer's body had become the receptacle for all those feelings he could not bear to voice. His hatred of himself and his hatred of his body had become fused, so that by altering the shape of his body he was communicating a desire to reshape every aspect of his mind. He was in thrall to an unconscious fantasy that by streamlining his body he was also streamlining his emotional world, riding himself of the shame and guilt that had preoccupied him since waking in the hotel room. The paradox of the evening's events was encoded in this body that he both hated and loved, the self that was both narcissistic and utterly consumed by self-hatred. He began the night with desire, a hope that his wish for a partner would be fulfilled. He was then faced with the disappointment of a lack of desire, a realisation that this stranger was not going to be his partner. And then there was a vicious guillotining of consciousness in which his desires were subsumed by those of his assailant in an attack that had been eradicated by a drug, an attack that could not be held in mind. As such, his body had to hold all that his mind could not.

Sexual abuse is an assault on the body as well as the mind. Studies have shown that survivors report significantly more medical concerns than people who have not experienced sexual abuse, the most frequent medial complaint being pelvic pain (Cunningham et al., 1988) followed by gastrointestinal problems, headaches, and difficulty swallowing (Ratican, 1992). It is often the body that houses the horrors that the mind cannot contain, transforming itself into a repository for unvoiced trauma. Through eating disorders and physical self-assaults, the survivors' body is at risk of becoming a lifelong receptacle of all the aggression, frustration, and hatred that should, rightfully, belong to the abuser. When the abuser is either physically absent or psychically protected from attack through the perversion of attachment, all the survivor may have left to hate is his own body.

Cultural influences on men's relationship with food

In placing the experience of being sexually abused at the genesis of some eating disorders, I do not wish to disregard the wide range of sociocultural issues that exert a growing influence on men who develop difficulties with food (Haworth-Hoeppner, 2000). Any consideration of what male survivors do with their bodies has to consider the complex changes in how we view the body of the male that have occurred over the past decade. It has generally been stated that gay men tend to be more dissatisfied with their bodies and may be at greater risk of developing symptoms of eating disorders compared to heterosexual men (Kaminski et al., 2005; Feldman & Meyer, 2007). Morgan and Arcelus (2009) conclude, however, that widespread body image dissatisfaction exists among younger men regardless of sexual orientation. Even a casual glance at male imagery in advertising, films, and computer gaming confirms the fact that all men are now prey to the kind of impossible body image ideals that have been assailing women and gay men for decades. The work of feminist psychoanalysts such as Susie Orbach (1978, 2005, 2009) has done much to alert us to the complex societal, cultural, and intrapsychic underpinnings of women's eating disorders, leaving a space to be filled in relation to the increasingly perverse and self-destructive ways that men are relating to their bodies. As Jones and Morgan state: "Socio-cultural constructs of eating disorders have been illuminated by feminist theory, but the lack of equivalent discourse addressing male gender identity has left our knowledge of eating disorders in men aetiolated" (2010, p. 29).

Forms of eating disorder

Jacobs (1986) argued that a psychological precondition must exist in order for a person to acquire an eating addiction. This included feelings of inadequacy, inferiority, low self-esteem, and a pervasive sense of rejection by parents. Jacobs found that the act of overeating did not only relieve anxiety but also brought on a dissociative-like state. Eating disorders have been stereotyped as a female disorder. Men's diets tend to strive towards a shape goal rather than a weight goal and, therefore, often do not meet the weight criteria of an eating disorder (Anderson et al., 2000). Men with bulimia look normal in terms of weight and diagnostic criteria tend to focus on female rather than male symptomology, such as the impact of eating disorders impact upon menstruation (Feltman & Ferraro, 2011). Eating disorders are divided into three diagnostic categories: anorexia nervosa, bulimia nervosa, and the atypical eating disorders. It should be noted, however, that the disorders have many features in common and patients frequently move between them (Fairburn & Harrison, 2003). In his study of the history of eating disorders in males, Silverman (1990) discovered three case reports between the years 1689 and 1790. All three cases describe incidents of anorexia nervosa long before the term was coined by Queen Victoria's physician a century later (Gull, 1874). Anorexia nervosa has the highest premature fatality rate of any mental illness and the highest suicide rate of any mental disorder (Strother et al., 2012).

Raudenbush and Zellner (1997) and Steinhausen (2002) concluded that men account for approximately ten per cent of those afflicted with some form of eating disorder. More recently Hudson, Hiripi et al. (2007) put the figure at somewhere between twenty-five and forty per cent. Carlat et al. (1997) estimated that ten to fifteen per cent of people with anorexia or bulimia are male. In their review of numerous studies, Mond et al. (2014) noted a higher male incidence when it came to subclinical eating disorders. Forty-two to forty-five per cent of those engaged in binge eating were male, as were twenty-eight to one hundred per cent of individuals who regularly purged. Laxative abuse among genders was nearly even, and fasting for weight loss was engaged in by nearly forty per cent of the males. Cox (2015) has argued that the rate of eating disorders in males has risen by twenty-seven per cent since 2000. Cohn (2013) argued that prevalence of eating disorders in males is greater than estimated because men are often too stigmatised to seek treatment for problems more commonly associated with women. Only sixteen per cent of men with eating disorders seek treatment (Freeman, 2005). As with women, the risk of developing anorexia peaks between the ages of ten and twenty-four (Currin et al., 2005).

Cafri, Yamamiya et al.'s (2005) tripartite aetiology of eating disorders clusters parental, peer, and media influences together as being instrumental in shaping attitudes towards our body image. Gendered self-perceptions have tended to privilege thinness for women and muscularity for men (Ricciardelli & McCabe, 2004). Nowell and Ricciardelli (2008) conclude that men tend to desire increased muscularity and reduced body fat, a desire that is different from that of women's for weight loss. A traumatogenic symptom that afflicts far more men than women is muscle dysmorphia and the abuse of steroids (Strother et al., 2012). Muscle dysmorphia—a pathological preoccupation with muscularity—is a variant of body dysmorphic disorder. It is also known as "reverse anorexia" and "bigorexia", produces a compulsive obsession with one's muscles and leanness (Leone et al., 2005), and is, according to Pope et al.'s (2005) study, associated with more severe forms of psychopathology than other types of body dysmorphic disorder. We are also seeing through our work with survivors such as Frazer more of what Jones and Morgan (2012) term "bulimorexia", the combination of both conditions.

Power and regression

Strother, Lemberg et al. (2012) highlighted the connection between sexual abuse and male eating disorders. At the heart of most eating disorders is an overwhelming desire to be in control (Kitson, 2012). Sexual abuse robs the survivor of a sense of power, agency, and autonomy, creating a pervasive sense of bodily and emotional impotence. When one's body has been entered into without one's consent, a sense of quasi-control can be attained by controlling whatever food is allowed in. There occurs in many survivors of male abuse a disturbing process of regression through which infantile defences are resurrected in order to deal with overwhelming anxieties. This connects with Anna Freud's (1936) concept of psychological defences involving a regression in which an individual deals with developmental anxiety by reverting to a lower level of development. In such cases we are working with a juxtaposition of the adult man and the small boy desperately warring to gain mastery over their bodily domain. An eating disorder provides the survivor with a way of hating and then attacking his body. The body becomes a receptacle of vicious, punitive projections in which the identities of the survivor and the perpetrator of abuse are fused. The abuse of food is an echo of the abuse of the body. By attacking the self the survivor is making a futile attempt to attack those who originally abused him.

Attacks on desire

A secondary gain for male survivors who starve their bodies is the resultant lowering of testosterone levels, leading to a low, or sometimes non-existent, libido. This provides the male survivor with respite from desire, a desire all too often infused with fear, self-hatred, and, perhaps most importantly of all, shame (Dorahy & Clearwater, 2012). Rørtveit et al. (2009) reflect on the pivotal role of shame in the lives of those who have experienced sexual abuse, a finding that my work with Frazer corroborated. In interpreting his eating and body distortions as defences against the shame of having been raped, it became more possible for Frazer to adopt a more nuanced perspective on his abuse. His view of it was originally a paranoid/schizoid one in which rape had reduced his world to a battlefield and his identity to that of victim. His defences were so tightly constructed that he could barely move. His sexual desire was frozen, his libido sublimated into his compulsive exercise, affording him a protective membrane against the threatened impingement of desire and sexuality. His sexual orientation remained a strong part of his identity; it was just that he was too terrified to act on it, desire having been devastatingly conflated with threat. He became increasingly aware of the sexual interest engendered by his muscular shape, and voiced a childlike curiosity about the contradiction inherent in being the object of sexual gazes having constructed a muscular wall against the desire of others. For him, obsessively controlled eating and bodybuilding were not attempts to sexualise himself. They were symptoms of his desire to desexualise himself, to place himself outside the confines of ordinary but potential annihilatory sexual need.

Asexuality as a defence

Wenninger (1998) concluded that childhood sexual abuse was linked with low levels of body esteem and sexual attractiveness, a finding echoed in the work of Eubanks, Kenkel, and Gardner (2006). Murray et al. (2008) traced the link between child sexual abuse and body image in their sample of reported self-harmers. Some of Frazer's symptoms can be read as attempts to annihilate desire—both his own and that of others. His retreat into a world without desire is a common response following an experience of sexual violation. In place of its associations with pleasure, creativity, and love, sex has become conflated with pain, violation, and destruction. It is placed closer to the death instinct than the pleasure principle. The libido becomes invested with fear and anxiety, leading to a state of bodily isolation in which desire is disavowed in favour of the supposed safety of asexuality. We should be aware that, in working with patients such as Frazer, we are faced with men for whom a different lexicon has been constructed with which to narrate their drastically altered view of sexuality and desire. Sex is no longer sex. It is violence, brutality, viciousness, and loss. It has to be defended against through a withdrawal from desire or, in those cases where trauma appears to trigger a state of hyper-arousal, an immersion in sexual compulsion (see Chapter Three).

Alcohol and drug use

The law in relation to sexual abuse is confused and complicated by alcohol and drugs. Their presence in cases can undermine the position of the victim in the criminal justice system and may be a causal factor underlying the high attrition rates in rape cases (Brown et al., 2007; Krahe et al., 2008). In several cases that have gone before the Criminal Injuries Compensation Authority, victims have had their compensation reduced because they had been consuming alcohol before they were raped (Gavin, 2013). The use of drugs and alcohol by the victim confuse the belief that, despite some changes, continues to shape legal responses to sexual crime: that "real rape" is an attack by a stranger on an unsuspecting victim who is overcome by force (Stewart et al., 1996).

Alcohol is the substance most often used in cases of rape and sexual assault (Slaughter, 2000; Hindmarch et al., 2001; Scott-Ham & Burton, 2005). The other drugs most often used in rape include gamma-hydroxybutyrate (GHB), gamma-butyrolactone (GBL), tranquilisers (including Valium and Rohypnol) and ketamine. The effects of such drugs include lowered inhibitions, difficulties in concentrating or speaking, loss of balance, difficulties in moving, blurred vision, amnesia, confusion and disorientation, paranoia, hallucinations, and nausea and vomiting. Rohypnol has proven particularly popular with rapists due to its potency in rendering the victim completely incapable of resisting. The effects start twenty to thirty minutes after taking the drug, peak within two hours and may persist for eight to twelve hours. A victim can be so incapacitated he collapses, eyes open, able to observe events but completely unable to move. Memories of the assault are blurred or, in some cases, absent.

Much like preverbal abuse in infanthood, when there are few words or memories with which to narrate the trauma, it is difficult for an adult to create a new, post-trauma narrative when the details of the attack are blurred by alcohol or drugs. Therapeutic progress tends to depend on the forming of a new narrative in which the victim can be relieved of his feelings of guilt and shame and be able to attribute them to the perpetrator. This is impeded when the original narrative is a blurred one. The usual feelings of guilt felt by many male survivors, their feelings that they, as men, should have been strong enough to resist their attacker, are magnified by the disinhibiting effects of drugs or alcohol. A new narrative has to be created.

The trauma of war

It is no coincidence that in describing my work with Frazer I have used the language of war, soldiering, and battlefields. Working with male survivors whose symptomology is dominated by eating disorders can easily take on an adversarial edge. In examining how the therapist's dissociative process can halt therapeutic progress, Bromberg writes:

> It becomes very easy to grow to hate the patient's eating disorder, and then without recognizing it, to hate that part of yourself that is trying but failing to cure it. The therapist begins to feel victimized by his own desire, and then feels the patient's pathology as an adversary … A transitional reality has to be constructed in which trust in human relatedness begins to become possible, and this can happen only through the therapist's surrender to his own dissociated self-experience. (Bromberg, 2006, p. 125)

Psychotherapy with eating-disordered male survivors does not just involve the meeting of two sets of the unconscious—that of the patient and that of the therapist. It is also the meeting of two bodies, with all that their differences convey. Despite our sessions taking place at times when I would not normally be hungry, I often left the consulting room feeling completely famished, desperate to fill myself up. At times my countertransference with Frazer was dominated by anxieties about my own body, which could feel so puny and underweight when compared with his. I wondered what he made of this key difference between us, whether he identified me as belonging to an opposing army, one that swore allegiance to a different set of body ideals. There were times when Frazer dared to put this curiosity into words, wondering whether I thought his bodily obsession was a form of madness, a purely narcissistic pathology or a way of avoiding thinking about what was going on inside his mind.

In truth it was all of these things, and more. No eating disorder has one foundation. The fact of his being raped with its particular narrative of drugged violence does not wholly explain why Frazer developed eating-related symptoms, whereas other victims of the same form of brutality may gravitate more towards depression, self-harm, or dissociation. As Goodsitt wrote:

> Eating disorders are symptomatic expressions that can occur in a relatively intact or structured psyche and reflect an internal conflict, or can occur in an undeveloped or incomplete mental structure and reflect a disorder of the self. The symptoms of an eating disorder can be either symbolic expressions of psychic aims and defences (drive-conflict model); symbolic representations (object relations model); or non-symbolic, restitutional emergency measures used to stem the tide of disrupted self-states threatened with the loss of cohesion of the self (self-psychological model). (1985, p. 207)

As with all symptomology associated with sexual abuse, the true processing of trauma cannot occur when only the symptom is examined. It has to examine the psychic structure underpinning the responses to trauma. For different therapists coming from different theoretical orientations this may be described as psychosexual stages, object relations, Jungian archetypes, the mirror stage, attachment models, etc. All theories are related ways of understanding the impact of infantile development on subsequent responses to trauma, and remind us of the need to adopt a binocular view of our work with male survivors, holding in mind the dual weights of early life experience and sexual violation.

The missing parts of the jigsaw

Frazer's memory of his rape was an incomplete one. Various pieces of the jigsaw would always remain tantalisingly absent from his mind. There are profound challenges to forming a therapeutic narrative when memory has been attacked by drugs, alcohol, or defence mechanisms such as dissociation. Faced with the difficulty of never knowing fully what his body had been subjected to, it is no surprise that Frazer was forced to reconstruct his body in lieu of reconstructing his narrative. The rebuilding of his body was one that involved elements of sadomasochism. The pleasure felt by the reconstruction was achieved through the pain of starvation, force-feeding, and bodily tortures. The healthy and ordinary pleasures of exercising and eating well were translated into a far more disturbing compulsion through which thought and reflection were disavowed. His capacity to look objectively into a mirror was altered by his highly distorted subjectivity. All he could see was a self that had to either be transformed or jettisoned. Many of his symptoms can be viewed as futile attempts to find a place of safety. By disavowing sex and desire he was building a fortress against the threat of abuse, a fear that underpinned so many of his interactions with the world. Breaking down the fortress required the building of trust and hope in his therapy, a long and arduous process that finally allowed him some relief from the isolated body he had constructed.

CHAPTER EIGHT

Physician heal thyself: the impact of trauma upon the clinician

In this chapter I wish to explore the potential toxicity of working with male survivors of abuse. This work is deeply challenging, demanding of its practitioners a capacity to tolerate painfully high levels of trauma, to the extent where we are bound to ask why we engage with such agonising, gruelling, and potentially debilitating work in the first place. In his paper "Are incest victims hated?" MacCarthy (1988) discusses his decision to stop working with patients who were survivors of incest. He talked to Alvin Rosenfeld, an American expert in the same field, who had stopped his own work, quite suddenly, after ten to twelve years, and concluded that working with incest victims induced a form of burnout. This resonated with MacCarthy, who felt his own decision to stop "may be my expression of unconscious hate, or of that pervasive and leaden sense of inner desolation I feel so often, a desolation which mirrors faithfully the inner desolation so well known to these patients" (1988, p. 120).

Winnicott's paper on "Hate in the counter-transference" (1949) describes the need to understand and tolerate those feelings of hate evoked in us by our patients. Winnicott is writing primarily in this paper about working with psychotic patients, but also touches on the presence of maternal ambivalence and hatred in the analysis of neurotic and hysterical patients: "A mother has to be able to tolerate hating her baby without doing anything about it" (1949, p. 74). Talking up the position of the analyst, he says, "However much he loves his patients he cannot avoid hating them, and fearing them, and the better he knows this the less will hate and fear be the motive determining what he does to his patients" (p. 69). Just as our patients can struggle to understand, tolerate, and process their ambivalence, so can we. The experience of sexual abuse produces a vulnerability to splitting; the most obvious split being that of the world into good and bad, with little tolerance for what may exist between the two. Real, authentic ambivalence necessitates the holding of something that abuse attacks—the capacity to hold two thoughts in mind. Love and hate can and should exist alongside each other, interacting and interconnecting in ways that change and modulate each state. Sexual abuse tends to reduce the capacity for depressive position functioning, magnifying instead a paranoid-schizoid view of the world in which experiences, thoughts, and feelings tend to be perceived as either cataclysmically bad or euphorically good. As has been seen in the preceding chapters, achieving and maintaining the depressive position is profoundly difficult for the pre-therapy survivor of abuse, as trauma has distorted the lens through which he views the world, robbing him of access to a nuanced encounter with emotions. Feelings are black and white, have tremendously sharp edges, and produce an ongoing oscillation between dread and dissociation that can ultimately result in psychic breakdown.

We are vulnerable as therapists and supervisors to similar splitting processes. Trauma is a bomb that detonates nearest to the survivor, but which also explodes into those around him. The kind of therapist we are depends on so many factors, including the kind of training we have undergone, the form of supervision we receive, and the kind of personality we have. In my study of forensic psychotherapy with disabled patients (Corbett, 2014) I examined Wilson et al.'s (1994) concept of the traumatofilic and the traumatophobic therapist in which encounters with survivors of trauma result in two extreme responses: excessive, unboundaried involvement in working with survivors or, on the other hand, an extreme avoidance of and distancing from them. Both types of therapist have a fundamental problem with empathy. For the traumatofilic therapist empathy is undiluted by thought, insight, and the capacity to work with the negative transference. The traumatophobic therapist disavows empathy, overlaying it with a surfeit of detachment and a tendency to focus solely on the negative at the cost of the positive. In addition to this being a function of the therapist's valency for certain attitudes, it should be viewed also in the context of projection—our vulnerability to receive and enact the most primitive splitting processes evacuated into us by our patients. These phenomena may be seen most vividly in group processes involving male survivors, where the tendency for splitting and projection are magnified by the clustering of manifold experiences of severe trauma. This vignette seeks to illustrate the weight of group processes and the extremely vulnerable position we as therapists occupy in the midst of such massified experiences.

* * *

"Tim" has been running a group for male survivors of sexual abuse for just over a year. This particular group was set up for men who experienced sexual abuse as children in boarding schools, and has been funded partly through a financial compensation scheme following a civil case against the school's governors. The group is run on a "slow open" model, meaning that it is a long-term, ongoing facility in which men spend varying amounts of time. At the point in this group's development that I will focus on in this vignette, it has a core membership of six men—four of whom have been attending since its beginning, the remaining two of whom have recently replaced men who have left the group.

Tim is a therapist whose work I have admired for some time, having previously supervised some of his individual work with male and female survivors of sexual abuse. I was pleased, initially, to be asked to supervise his group work, and felt confident of his capacity to facilitate a group that would provide a space in which the processing of individual and communal trauma could take place. Since then I have been surprised by how much the group appears to have unravelled him, to the point where I am beginning to have concerns about the efficacy of his continuing to conduct it.

We begin today's supervision session with an absence—Tim is ten minutes' late when he eventually arrives. He is breathless and apologetic, launching into an account of how his printer had broken down at the last minute, depriving him of the chance to print out his notes for supervision. He voices his anger at his organisation for failing to resource him properly in his work, and rails against the funding cuts that he fears are preventing true therapeutic work from happening in his setting. I point out that this is not the first time he has arrived without notes, making me wonder if there are aspects of the group content that are too painful to document and share. Tim is clearly angry at this interpretation, reminding me that "real life" gets in the way sometimes—not everything should be subject to psychoanalytic interpretation.

Having been put in my place, I invite Tim to tell me how the last group has been. What follows is a disjointed, somewhat rambling account of the group. It began with several absences caused by latecomers. One of the men voiced his anxieties that the group may not survive, that lateness and absence had become much more marked lately. Another group member disparaged this view, saying that, "It is what it is—people are stuck in traffic or on the tube. Why worry about them?" A couple of latecomers then arrived, full of rage about the unreasonable time the group was scheduled, making it impossible to avoid traffic hold-ups.

Tim hesitates here, unable to remember what happened next. I wonder what he had done with the rather aggressive attack on the group boundaries—had he interpreted it? Tim says he had decided not to; it would have felt like a defensive attack. Instead he took up the concrete reality being presented, an ongoing complaint about the timing of the group. This elicited much agreement from the group, most of whom expressed their desire for the time to be changed to a more sensible one. One man, one of the two relative newcomers to the group, expressed his foreboding about the time changing, given he had worked hard with his employers to negotiate time off.

This led into a discussion about whether the group was worth continuing with or not. Three of the men said they had been debating this for some time (the inference being that these debates had been taking place outside the group), and were reaching the conclusion that the effort required to come to the group simply wasn't worth it. Tim tried to say something about how hard it usually is to have to face painful emotional issues, but this got submerged under a tide of discussion about the practicalities of the group. I ask Tim to talk more about what he was feeling at this point. He says that he experienced feelings of worthlessness and despair, and, indeed, found himself identifying with the men's sense that the group may not survive. Tim grows quite emotional at this point, saying that for some time he has felt that the group isn't giving the men what they need, and that perhaps he is the wrong person to conduct it. In an earlier session, Tim had disclosed his own history of sexual abuse, and at this point in the supervision session he refers back to it, saying that he has himself been facing doubts about his own therapy, whether it is really addressing the impact of his history upon him. He hints at difficulties in his relationship that have become exacerbated since the group began.

Tim describes the group as ending quite chaotically—two of the men saying they had to leave early, and one man beginning to talk about his history of abuse in great detail, just minutes before the group was due to end. Tim found himself "caught in the headlights", and the group overran by five minutes. The man disclosing appeared extremely distressed at this point, and Tim reports feeling overwhelmed by concern about his well-being since the session. As Tim draws to the end of his account of the session, I look at the clock, noticing we are ourselves in danger of overrunning, leaving little space to think together about what is going on between Tim, his group, and me.

* * *

Vicarious traumatisation

In supervising this group experience I found myself having to attend not just to what was happening to the men in the group, but, just as importantly, what was happening to Tim. This is not just the story of a group in crisis, it is also that of a therapist being consumed by the toxicity of the clinical material. The interplay between the trauma experienced by the men and the internal world of the therapist had produced a state of mind that can best be described as vicarious traumatisation. This term was first used by McCann and Pearlman (1990) to describe a particular set of changes that occur within clinicians over time as a result of working with patients who have experienced sexual trauma. These include pervasive changes in the clinician's sense of self and of the world, manifesting in difficulties in interpersonal relationships and resulting in other dysfunctional behaviours. McCann and Pearlman felt that the concept of countertransference was too narrow to describe the specific impact upon the therapist that comes from working with victims of sexual abuse—the "lasting alterations in (the therapist's) cognitive schema … [that have a] significant impact on the therapists' feelings, relationships, and life" (1990, p. 136). In *Trauma and the Therapist*, Pearlman and Saakvitne describe vicarious trauma as "a process through which the therapist's inner experience is negatively transformed through empathic engagement with clients' trauma material" (1995a, p. 279). In their paper "Treating therapists with vicarious traumatisation and secondary traumatic stress" (Pearlman & Saakvitne, 1995b) they describe two sets of factors that contribute to vicarious traumatisation:

1. Specific characteristics of the therapy and its context, including characteristics of the clients; the nature of the work itself; and the political, social, and cultural context within which both the traumatic events and the therapy take place.
2. Particular characteristics and vulnerabilities of the therapist and the way he or she works.

Gartner (2014) suggests the more interpersonal term "countertrauma", a phrase that builds on Wolstein's (1988) notions of transference and countertransference, anxiety and counteranxiety, resistance and counterresistance. "In this spirit", writes Gartner, "I am speaking of trauma and countertrauma, implying a fluid, intersubjective, two-person system, rather than 'vicarious traumatisation', which seems to imply a one-person model, with trauma residing first in the patient, then transferring to the analyst, both distinct from countertransference" (2014, p. 612).

It was my view that Tim was not "burnt out". It is important to note Canfield's (2005) finding that vicarious traumatisation and worker burnout are distinctly different processes that clinicians need to differentiate between, even though they are often similar in their initial presentation. Burnout is a response to the general psychological stress of working with difficult situations, and can occur in any profession. The term describes a general feeling of being overloaded and progresses gradually as a result of emotional exhaustion, with the burnout not necessarily being linked to specific clinical issues. Vicarious trauma is a response to particular trauma-related phenomena, and occurs only among those who work specifically with trauma survivors. It carries greater psychological weight, leading not just to the removal of energy and motivation that burnout induces, but to deeply embedded shifts in feelings of trust, control, intimacy, and safety. The two phenomena share characteristics, can appear, on the surface, to be similar, and can both result in profound dips in the quality of clinical care provided.

Does working with sexual abuse threaten the stability and health of non-clinicians? Little research has been done into the impact of vicarious trauma on other professionals dealing with issues of sexual abuse outside the clinical sphere. One study into lawyers working with domestic violence and family law found that the lawyers demonstrated significantly higher levels of traumatic stress and burnout compared to two control groups of mental health providers and social services workers (Levin & Greisberg, 2003). This study concluded that the symptoms related to solicitors with extremely high caseloads and a lack of supervision around trauma and its effects. In an earlier study police officers were found to have significantly higher symptoms of psychological distress (including anxiety, depression, dissociation, and sleep problems) and PTSD symptoms than mental health professionals (Follette et al., 1994). Regardless of discipline, it is clear that, without adequate structures of holding and containment, all those working with issues of sexual abuse are vulnerable to toxic effects.

Countertransference

Countertransference is also related to, while being different from, vicarious trauma. It has evolved since its first rather ambivalent formulation by Freud (1910a) when he viewed it as being a purely personal problem for the analyst. It is a concept that came to describe those unconscious reactions to a patient that stem from the analyst's own history and unconscious, and one that also came to include the analyst's unconscious erotic or hostile feelings towards the patient that, if unchecked and unanalysed, interfered with the objectivity of the analytic work. A more positive paradigm emerged through the course of the twentieth century, with countertransference being viewed increasingly as an aid rather than a hindrance to understanding the unconscious world of the patient. Contemporary psychoanalytic views of the countertransference take an intersubjective perspective in which the phenomenon is viewed as a jointly created one that has tremendous diagnostic and treatment uses, while also requiring careful monitoring to ensure it does not become too diluted by what Fordham (1960) called "illusory countertransference". By this, he meant a too personal and narrow reading of countertransference processes by which the role of the patient's unconscious narrative is overshadowed by that of the analyst.

Vicarious trauma almost invariably involves countertransference issues but is not inevitably part of the countertransference process. As with the concept of burnout, the two paradigms are similar and have some overlap, but are also different. Countertransference, for example, tends to emanate directly from what happens within the clinical session. While it can certainly stay with the therapist after the session has ended, it has its genesis in the therapeutic encounter. Vicarious trauma transcends the confines of the consulting room, finding a home in many other places. Vicarious traumatisation has been demonstrated to be both a cumulative process, building up over a long period of time through the volume and range of cases being dealt with (Conrad, 2011), while also being brought about very quickly by a single case. The latter phenomenon may be seen in the profound impact upon social workers of working with the deaths of children such as James Bulger or Peter Connelly (Tehrani, 2011).

A paradox lies at the heart of attempts to protect against vicarious traumatisation. A frequently cited form of protection against it is professional experience (Hoff et al., 2009; Conrad, 2011)—the cumulative wisdom accrued from extensive experience of working with trauma building up a set of healthy defences. And yet the opposite may also be true: the more we work with sexual trauma the less likely we are to notice its cumulative impact upon us, and the more likely we are to fall prey to its unconscious effects. This was one of the elements of my supervision of Tim that was initially confusing. He was a highly experienced clinician in whom I had great faith in his capacity to work with high levels of sexual trauma. And yet it may be that this experience served to disable his capacity to work with this group. Tim's difficulties with grasping the unconscious drama unfolding in this particular session illustrate a phenomenon that is often present in this work—whether it be individual or group psychotherapy—that of countertrauma. Through the supervision of this group it became clear that a complex two-way intersubjective process was unfolding, by which the men's trauma served to activate that of Tim, and vice versa. He was, at times, capable of losing his role as therapist—becoming instead a group member, thinking and reacting as concretely as the other group members.

Failed dependency

The specific characteristics of this particular group and its context had a profound impact upon its progress, and serve to remind us of the importance of a therapeutic point of view that is not focused wholly upon the internal world but can also take notice of the external. The fact of this group being financed through a compensation scheme following a civil case forms part of the group matrix. It is hard to think of this fact without being aware of the varying reactions to it that might be held by the men: relief that the school has taken some form of responsibility for the original abuses, shame at being the recipient of charity, anger at what could be seen as an attempt by the school to buy forgiveness. Unless these reactions can be made conscious, interpreted, and processed (something Tim found difficult to do), it is likely they will exacerbate the core ambivalence brought by the men into the group in the first place.

Clues as to this group's, and Tim's, problems with authority may be glimpsed in the cavalier way in which he treated supervision. It had become something of an annoyance to him, something he could be late and unprepared for, as if it were a hindrance rather than a help to his therapeutic work. No surprise then that this was echoed by the men's ambivalence towards the group itself. This is a common phenomenon in working with male survivors, given the deeply embedded feelings of shame carried by the majority of patients, alongside the rage at the abuser. Shame underscores the notion of victimhood. The anger at the world communicated by the men in Tim's group (the world taking the form of the useless, dysfunctional group; the chaotic transport system; and the impotent figure of Tim) did not do what anger should do. It did not relieve the men of their impotence, nor did it make them feel more powerful. Perhaps if Tim had been able to receive and process the anger on their behalf it may have. Instead, he colluded in the group notion that the men had been abused by the world, meaning that the world was wrong. And the world, for the men, was equated with authority. Authority had failed them, and had, of course, to be attacked at every opportunity.

The concept of failed dependency is one that is particularly apposite in looking at the functions of a group such as this where the therapist has come to symbolise all those who have previously failed the men (Hopper, 2003). It is a concept that has a wider application to all therapeutic work with survivors, articulating as it does the particularly fraught relationship the survivor can have with those who represent authority. These figures are subject to powerful projections from the survivor, personifying through the transference all those who are felt to have turned a blind eye towards the abuse inflicted on the patient. This form of projective identification does not only find its way into the dynamics of the therapist/patient dyad, it can colour and shape a vast matrix of interrelationships surrounding the survivor. Even the most benign of attachments can be experienced as representing aspects of the abuser. Partners can be experienced as siblings within an incestuous family, who know but cannot bear to talk about the abuse unfolding before their eyes. Friends can be related to as colluders, passively allowing rape and sexual assault to be enacted, uninterested in calling it to a halt. Even strangers can find themselves unknowingly recruited into this powerful projective process, becoming experienced as if they are representatives of the societal world that has allowed abuse to continue unacknowledged, unreported, and unstopped.

Organisations are also subject to the impact of failed dependency. In some ways it has been helpful to be a psychotherapist operating outside the remit of an organisation, as the organisation can be experienced by the survivor as an abusive entity, related to in paranoid and aggressive ways. This is not to say that the therapist will not be on the receiving end of the negative transference. This is part and parcel of the therapeutic process. There is, however, something particularly seductive for the survivor in the fantasy that an organisation represents his abuser. He can hate the organisation (be it the government, social services, the media) without having to engage in an individual battle. It is, however, important that we also acknowledge the other side of this coin, the potential for the organisation to be experienced in a more benign way. The French psychoanalyst Henri Rey often spoke of the "brick mother" when describing his positive attachment, and that of his patients, to the place in which therapy took place. Patients will sometimes need to form secure attachments to their therapeutic surroundings, allowing the negative to be directed at the therapist.

Impact of the gender and sexuality of the therapist

A complex set of personal circumstances (relationship breakdown, personal trauma history being re-triggered) disabled Tim to a profound extent, meaning that his capacity to withstand the attacks of the group was compromised. He became, instead of the authoritative, solid, containing therapist, another group member, at risk of being re-traumatised by the group material. As a clinician, it is possible and often essential to make use of one's own history of trauma in order to help our patients. Here, however, creativity was attacked by a form of counter-trauma that threatened to rob the group of its potential for healing and recovery. In reflecting on Tim's work with his group, I found myself wondering how different this experience would have been had the therapist been female. Most research into the impact of working with sexual abuse tends to focus on work with women. For example, Schauben and Frazier (1995) researched the impact upon female psychologists of their work with female survivors. Those who had a high percentage of survivors in their caseload reported higher levels of vicarious trauma, particularly disrupted beliefs about the goodness of other people and more symptoms of post-traumatic stress disorder. VanDeusen and Way's (2006) study into vicarious trauma uncovered a profound impact of the clinical work on therapists' attitudes towards sex, sexuality, and relationships, with the notion of sexual intimacy becoming tainted by close proximity to those whose experiences of sex had been suffused with trauma.

The question of whether it is better for a man rather than a woman to work with male survivors tends to be considered in very concrete ways. Owen et al.'s comprehensive (2009) study into the impact of therapist gender on clinical efficacy found that gender was *not* related to psychotherapy outcomes. Some psychotherapists were better at treating men, whereas others were better at treating women, but there was no evidential correlation between positive outcome and whether the therapist was male or female. To accede to the patient's request to see either a male or a female therapist is not as simple or as empowering as it might appear. A wish for a kind of adhesive mirroring can lie beneath a patient's desire to see someone who is as much like them as possible—same gender, age, and sexual orientation. I worry that too automatic an accession to these kind of desires can rob the therapy of its capacity to work through and process what lies at the heart of difference—the complex interweaving of curiosity, frustration, hope, envy, and desire that should lie at the heart of the therapeutic dyad. Assessing the request for the therapist to mirror the patient's life experiences is also an assessment of the patient's capacity to work more in the symbolic than the concrete.

Desire for mirroring

Many homosexual patients wish to only see a homosexual therapist, a request that is often symptomatic of a general fear that a heterosexual therapist would be vulnerable to a form of pathologising homophobia that has been the hallmark of certain brands of psychotherapy (Lewes, 1988). A male patient might only wish to see a male therapist in the hope that something problematic about masculinity and self may be implicitly understood and, thus, not necessarily looked at. Conversely, a male patient may ask to see a woman, fearing the shame that exposing their experiences of powerlessness to another man might evoke, or the sexual desire that might emerge between them. With those "worried well" patients who come into therapy without the history of abuse that male survivors bring with them, the transference tends only to emerge once the therapeutic work has begun. With survivors of sexual trauma there is a far greater propensity for a pre-treatment transference to take hold even before therapist and patient have laid eyes upon one another. For the worried well patient there will be fantasies about the therapist—some internet searches may be undertaken, some questions at initial telephone enquiry stage about their training, experience, and ways of working. For the neurotic patient these pre-therapy struggles are normal and appropriate. What tends to be absent from this stage for the patient who has not been abused is an edge of paranoia and terror that can often grip the survivor.

There can be an expectation that the therapist will be an abuser and that something dreadful will happen once the consulting room door is opened. So the drive for healing, the need to find some reparation from the ongoing agony of abuse, clashes with the unconscious expectation that instead of healing there will be hurt, that wounds will be not only be opened but sustained. This accounts for the tremendously powerful ambivalence that stops some potential patients from ever seeking therapy, slows down the search for others (sometimes by years), and undercuts much of the therapeutic process. Ambivalence, in its myriad forms, becomes the third object in the room, making the dyad into a triad and requiring of both therapist and patient the capacity to bear and ultimately understand and process the curious amalgam of desire and fear that colours the transference relationship. The desire for sameness, for a therapist who is "just like me", can be a way of negating ambivalence, but it tends not to work. The desire by the patient for an enmeshed, symbiotic relatedness, and the wish on the part of the therapist to fulfil that desire, produces an unhealthy and unrealistic idealisation, a risk of over-identification that can, if unchecked, lead to a painful therapeutic failure. As Kohut (1971) demonstrated in his work on narcissism, idealisation of the self and of the therapist can be allowed during therapy, but has to gradually diminish as a result of unavoidable optimal frustration.

The fourth basic assumption

Of the various safeguards that need to be in place to ensure therapists are not traumatised by working with the toxicity of male sexual abuse, supervision is perhaps one of the most important. As previously noted, to have a clinical caseload that is too full of abuse cases increases the risk of vicarious traumatisation (Bell et al., 2003). Paradoxically, the more experienced clinicians become, the more abuse cases are referred to them, leading to a heightened vulnerability to becoming overwhelmed by the toxicity contained within each case. Any clinic or organisation working predominantly with sexual abuse is as vulnerable as the individuals within it to vicarious trauma. Hopper's (2003) theory of the fourth basic assumption is a useful paradigm in understanding this vulnerability, as it reveals the tendency of groups (and thus organisations) to respond to internal and external threats to their existence in ways that, while experienced on an individual level, are felt more powerfully on a group level.

Sexual abuse is a trauma that is incredibly difficult to process, and tends to result in splitting processes. On an individual level, these may be manifested in paranoid-schizoid functioning, dissociative states, or other extreme fragmentations of the psyche. McCoy articulates Hopper's theory of trauma in organisations most clearly when she writes:

> Basic assumption incohesion describes a process of oscillation between the bi-polar states of aggregation and massification that results when a group and/or its members suffer trauma, which arises from failed dependency on people or situations. In this process, a group deteriorates into an aggregate (a collection of minimally connected people) whose members suffer anxieties based on isolation and lack of safety, which become so severe that the

> aggregate shifts to become a mass (a collection of people with maximal mutual attraction and little individuation) wherein its members now suffer merger-related anxieties such as fear of suffocation. The anxieties associated with massification precipitate a shift back to aggregation and a non-developmental oscillation between aggregation and massification ensues. (2012, pp. 89–90)

One visible sign of these processes is the tendency of some organisations to adopt a stance of inauthentic cohesion. The pain of the abuse with which they work is defended against through the adoption of a manic disavowal of difference. This is the organisation whose members all think alike. The complexity of sexual trauma is reduced to a simplistic black and white position. All those inside the organisation—victims, workers, and those who are both—are good, while all those outside (or perceived to be outside) are bad. Patients are regarded as a mass more than as a group of individuals. Their symptoms are seen as conforming to a checklist. There is an organisational transference to the imagined survivor whose characteristics (shame, vulnerability, hurt) are idealised and whose less acceptable symptoms (rage, arousal, excitement) are denigrated or misunderstood. This also tends to be the organisation that is vulnerable itself to acting out in dysfunctional ways, that has a valency towards scapegoating those of its members who dare to question the aggregated cult of the organisation, and that lurches from crisis to crisis in ways that mirror uncannily the pathologies of its most disturbed patients.

Any organisation predicated upon the treatment of people who have been sexually abused requires particular help, usually in the form of an external consultant, to help it deal with those sexually traumatogenic processes that get projected from the individual to the organisational, and back again. One of the unconscious questions that debilitate many organisations, is how to deal with their ambivalence. Sexual abuse is what it has been created (or how it has evolved) to deal with—a horrific and horrifying phenomenon that serves to dilute even the purest of philanthropic motives. I am worried when the representatives of any organisation find themselves idealising both the organisation and its clients. We need to be alarmed by the notion of "pioneering", "devoted", and "special" agencies that claim a wholly unique way of working with trauma, often thereby denigrating other agencies whose methodologies differ from their own. The organisation has thereby become over-identified with the ill rather than the healthy aspects of its patients—drawn to and reflecting paranoid-schizoid processes, and disavowing depressive position functioning and thinking.

The role of group therapy

Group therapy with male survivors should not be regarded as an opportunity for men to have individual psychotherapy alongside each other. The two ways of working are different and require different skills from the therapist. Group therapy is a process that, unlike individual processes, allows for a horizontal rather than purely vertical set of exchanges to take place. While individual work contains so much potential for reparative work to be done on the (often damaged) parental dyad, a group allows for sibling dynamics to enter the picture as well. It can be particularly helpful for those men whose experiences of sexual trauma have left them with a terrible conviction that they are the only survivor in the world. The pain of isolation is one that can be diluted by being with other survivors, enabling a realisation that, as unique and individual as every experience of sexual abuse is, there is much to be gained from the sharing of some of its commonalities.

Tim's drowning in the midst of this group is a reminder to us all about the dangers of this work. There is a toxicity encapsulated in the men's various experiences of sexual violation that can sink into our pores. Supervision is one of many elements of a support system, which have to be in place to prevent burnout or breakdown. A balanced (not purely abused-focused) practice, alongside a healthy non-work life also contribute to our capacity to carry and contain the trauma of our patients. Countertransference is not simply a way of understanding the projections of our patients, it is a barometer of our own mental states.

Vicarious resilience

I would like to end this chapter on a positive note. Not every patient I work with has pushed me down the road of vicarious traumatisation. On the contrary, I have gained huge amounts of pleasure from much of my work, finding myself approaching sessions with desire rather than dread. In their study, Hernandez et al. (2007) introduced the concept of vicarious resilience. Their research highlighted the emergence of resilience in the narratives of highly traumatised patients. By focusing on how therapists had both worked with and been affected by their patients' ability to respond to trauma in creative and powerful ways, this study noted the ways in which the patients' resilience was transmitted to and internalised by the psychotherapist—a useful counter to the traditional notion of vicarious traumatisation. If one side of the trauma coin can be felt, why not the other?

This notion has also been touched on in the work of Pearlman and Saakvitne (1995) and Schauben and Frazier (1995), with Brady et al.'s (1999) study of 1,000 female psychotherapists concluding that therapists with a greater exposure to patients who had been sexually traumatised ranked high on levels of "spiritual wellbeing" (a factor—articulated in varying forms of spiritual, secular, existential, and clinical language—often claimed to be damaged in working with trauma). In *Trauma and Recovery* (1992) Herman describes her view of the positive impact of working with patients who have been severely traumatised:

> Therapists who work with survivors report appreciating life more fully, taking life more seriously, having a greater scope of understanding of others and themselves, forming new friendships and deeper intimate relationships, and feeling inspired by the daily examples of their patients' courage, determination and hope. This is particularly true of those who, as a result of their work with patients, become involved in social action. These therapists report a sense of higher purpose in life and a sense of camaraderie that allows them to maintain a kind of cheerfulness in the face of horror. By constantly fostering the capacity for integration, in themselves and their patients, engaged therapists deepen their own integrity. (1992, p. 153)

The therapeutic process may not simply be beneficial for our patients, it may be imbuing us with something equally reparative and good.

CHAPTER NINE

The disunited states: working with dissociation

"Eric" slumps onto the couch, only he is not Eric. Today it is "John" who is starting the session. Eric is in his early forties, a strikingly good-looking man who works in the City. John is a sullen twelve-year-old who hates his sessions with me, detests the room we are in, would rather be doing anything than talking to his therapist. Eric and John share a body, and manage between them to let me know exactly which of them will be working with me on any particular day. Eric holds his body erect, his posture straight, his hands clasped tightly together, every inch of him the controlled, meticulous professional working hard to keep at bay anything that might betray his chaotic, tortured internal world.

"Thought I wasn't seeing you today," says John, his cockney accent far removed from Eric's carefully mannered tones. "Thought you were away." He picks at the fabric of the couch with a violent determination, mirroring the intensity with which he often picks at his own skin in sessions.

"I wonder why you thought that," I reply. "We don't have a break for a few months."

John ignores my response. "Sick of coming anyway. Just a waste of fucking time. Don't know what you're meant to do. Thought your job was to make us feel better. That's not working. You don't do nothing to stop me remembering. I remember all the time. What they did to me."

John does not need to explain that he is referring to his and Eric's memories of being sexually abused by a paedophile ring. The ring was led and co-ordinated by his parents, in conjunction with a group of at least eight neighbours and friends, men and women. Some, including his parents, ended up in prison. Others evaded justice, tormenting Eric with their continuing freedom. Despite the chaos of most of the rest of their lives, his parents applied a detailed methodology to Eric's abuse. It was regimented, ritualised, and severe, incorporating anal and oral abuse, torture, and several near-death experiences of which parts of him retain vivid memories. Eric was the direct victim of this abuse, and in the course of surviving it found himself fragmenting into various identities as a way of protecting himself from the agonising torture that for over six years became part of his daily life. John and various other selves were created to hold some of the most overwhelming memories so that Eric did not need to.

For some time John continues to berate me, before being interrupted by another self inhabiting Eric's body. The switch from self to self is seamless, with a shift in facial expression, tone of voice, and body posture indicating that another part of Eric's fragmented psyche has come to the fore. This time it is "Roddy", a frightened five-year-old who wants to apologise to me on behalf of John. "He doesn't mean it," he whispers, his voice shaking with fear. "He's scared. We're all scared. He remembers all the bad things the people did. The bad people. I remember too. Will they come back? Will they hurt us again?" He whimpers, more like a frightened animal than a child. I reassure Roddy that he is safe now, that the bad people can't get close to him again. He nods, then begins to tell me a story he has thought up in the few days since our last session. The story concerns a goldfish that gets dropped into the ocean by mistake, where he is terrorised by all sorts of strange other fish, determined to eat him alive. The story carries within it the residue of Eric's abuses, here crystallised by Roddy into the safe metaphor of fiction. As Roddy finishes the story, John returns, telling me that I am crazy to listen to Roddy's story—"He just wants to make it all nice," he shouts, his voice heavy with pain. "I'm the only one who's got the guts to tell you what they did to me. How the men stuck their pricks into me, how the women wanked me off, made me lick them out—all the things they did." He carries on for some time, and I seek to affirm his bravery in daring to use powerful words to impart a powerful, and unbearable, truth.

It takes time for me to realise that it is not Roddy who is staring, open mouthed at me, his eyes dull and unfocused. It is "Stranger", a self that has only recently begun to enter the session. His entrance is always like this—sudden, unexpected, and silent. He stares at me with his frighteningly empty gaze for some time, boring into me with a strange kind of lifeless intensity, a lustre that makes me think of how hungry this self, whoever it may be, however old or damaged it is, how hungry it is for something I do not seem able to provide. Roddy pops back, saying that Stranger is still trying to learn how to speak—he's really young; he isn't sure how to make sounds or form words. But when he does, Roddy assures me, I will know about it.

Eric suddenly comes forward, noting the lack of time we have left. "I've only just arrived—I presume the little ones have been talking to you." I let him know who has, and Eric nods, saying that he has mixed feelings about this. "I'm glad they came forward, but we never have time for me. Sometimes it's like I hardly see you." At this, we are out of time and he leaves, fastening his tie and straightening himself up to face the outside world once more. He sighs deeply, and something of his air of defeat and fear enters me, leaving me with a profound feeling of despair—a familiar feeling when working with him. How on earth, I wonder, does he manage the transition from the intensity of the consulting room to the demands of the office he goes to as soon as our sessions come to an end? How does he manage to silence these myriad selves (there are many others, some of whom have come into sessions, some of whom I have only been told about) in order to live his life?

* * *

There are men, like Eric, who challenge the most experienced of clinicians, whose experiences of trauma have resulted in symptoms that suggest they are untreatable. Many of the most extreme forms of sexual abuse remain unencoded within the psyche. They may have occurred at the pre-verbal stage of a boy's life, or simply be too saturated with horror to be able to be put into words. Stern uses the term "unformulated experience" (Stern, 2013) to describe those experiences that lay beyond the reach of verbal symbolisation. In using this term, Stern refers just as much to the benign as the malign. He describes the capacity to dissociate as being a vital milestone in the development of the psyche, and only ascribes pathological factors to it when it is more clearly a response to trauma. In order to cope with sexual abuse, survivors dissociate to avoid assimilating the full impact of the traumatic event (Elmone et al., 1996).

Dissociative identity disorder

The first case of dissociative identity disorder (DID) was thought to be described by Paracelsus in 1646 (Bliss, 1986) and, despite a long history, DID remains a divisive diagnosis. Opinions as to the aetiology of DID fall broadly into two models. The first is the *post-traumatic model*, which states a correlation between the frequency of DID and childhood trauma, suggesting that dissociation is a way of coping with the trauma experienced (Ross et al., 2008). The other is the *sociocognitive model*, in which a number of factors, including social cues, influence from psychotherapists, and personality type of the individual, contribute to the diagnosis of DID (Spanos, 1994). Gleaves (1996) re-examined the evidence for the latter model and concluded that it was based on numerous false assumptions about the psychopathology, assessment, and treatment of DID, and stated that there was no reason to doubt the connection between DID and childhood trauma. He further stated that treatment recommendations that follow from the sociocognitive model may be harmful because they involve ignoring the post-traumatic symptomatology of patients with DID.

It almost goes without saying that DID is a controversial diagnosis, eliciting the highest levels of scepticism that, decades ago, were reserved for the notion of child sexual abuse itself. Neuroscientific research is, fortunately, catching up with the clinical accounts of pioneers in the field, such as Kluft (1984a, 1984b), Sinason (1994, 2002), and Sachs and Galton (2008). The anatomical localisation of self-awareness and the brain mechanisms involved in consciousness were investigated by Reinders, Nijenhuis et al. (2003) through the functional neuroimaging of different emotional mental states of core consciousness in patients with DID. They demonstrated specific changes in localised brain activity consistent with the ability to generate at least two distinct mental states of self-awareness, each with its own access to autobiographical trauma-related memory. Their findings also revealed the existence of different regional cerebral blood-flow patterns for different senses of self. Vermetten, Schmal et al. (2006) examined hippocampal and amygdalar volumes in patients with DID using magnetic resonance imaging to measure the volumes of the hippocampus and amygdala in control groups of DID patients and non-DID subjects. Hippocampal volume was 19.2 per cent smaller and amygdalar volume was 31.6 per cent smaller in the patients with DID, compared to the healthy subjects. Diseth's (2005) research also clarifies a neurobiological basis to the complex symptomatology observed in dissociative patients. Similar results were examined by Tsai et al. (1999).

According to DSM-V, DID results in the presence of two or more distinct identities or personality states, alongside dissociative amnesia, dissociative fugue, and depersonalisation disorder. One patient may present with a number of fragmented selves—some of which may have little or no awareness of each other, their memories and sets of knowledge divided into watertight compartments. Time is also a problem for DID patients: minutes, hours, or days can become "lost" as one self comes forward, forcing other selves to retreat (Coleman, 2002).

Time and credibility

Time was a major issue for Eric's treatment. The session outlined above was a double one, lasting 100 minutes. The rationale for this was practical as much as clinical: fifty minutes was too short a time for the various selves embedded in Eric's psyche to come forward—let alone for Eric himself (his core self). Because one of the consequences of severe trauma of the kind experienced by Eric can be a disturbance in perceptual time functions, survivors' accounts of events in their life, including the details of their abuse, may contain descriptive inaccuracies (Hart & Steele, 1997). This impacts upon the therapist, placing inevitable strain upon the credibility we attach to our patient's memories and narratives. In Eric's case, he understood that my primary role was not a judicial one—I was there to help decode traumatic symptoms rather than to be an arbiter of truth. This was far harder for several other of his selves to accept. John returned frequently to one of his mantra-like questions: "So, do you think I'm making it all up then?" This was a difficult question to answer authentically, particularly when it followed, for example, a new account of being abused by members of a hip-hop band—an account that contained glaring inaccuracies and contradictions. John had a finely tuned ear for obfuscation, and tended to pre-empt my responses by saying, "I know you're gonna say you believe bad things have happened to me, but sometimes my brain gets mixed up about who did them and when. Well, that's just bullshit. You don't believe me!" This could then be followed by John physically leaving the consulting room, sometimes not returning for a number of sessions, leaving me uncertain as to his safety or, indeed, survival.

Amnesia

Childhood sexual abuse often involves partial or total amnesia regarding the details of the abuse, leading to a dissociation from sensations and affect (Braun, 1989). The fact that memories of the abuse, where it occurred, and when, can be blurred or missing from the patient's mind, unfortunately strengthens the arguments of bodies such as the False Memory Society, adding weight to their claims that the narratives of abuse presented by patients are more likely to be delusional, psychotic, or manufactured than attempts to communicate a truthful, if inaccurately recalled, memory. It is important, however, not to be drawn into this kind of false dichotomy of truth versus fiction. There have been times when I have had to take the risk of letting a patient know that the fact I think he is getting some of the details of his abuse "wrong" does not impair my ability to believe that the most dreadful abuses have been experienced by him. This may be understood by those parts of the patient that have more capacity for reflective functioning, while being wholly rejected by those parts that can only hear such a statement as a declaration of war.

The tightrope we walk when working with patients with DID is a precarious one. Working with any survivors of sexual abuse means that, at some points during the treatment we will be experienced not just as the abuser but (more troublingly, in many respects) as the collusive, passive bystander who turned a blind eye, who chose not to believe. We have to pay extremely close attention to the functions of countertransference in these kind of situations. In working with Eric there were times when I did find myself disbelieving many of the events his selves reported, being so full of bizarre and perverse detail. In seeking to understand my responses I had to wonder whether I was simply relieving myself of the agony of belief. If such grotesque, perverse, and revolting acts could be inflicted upon a child, what did it say about the humanity of which I was a part? Through this work—far more so than any work with patients without DID—I have found myself pulled into an ongoing debate as to the veracity of some of the accounts presented to me. I have envied those colleagues more able to simply believe their patients, knowing how tightly attuned our patients are to any shades of scepticism filtering through our attempts at a broadly supportive therapeutic stance.

Briere and Conte's (1993) research into the repression of sexual abuse incidents studied 450 adult clinical subjects reporting sexual abuse histories, of whom 267 identified some period in their lives, before the age of eighteen, when they had no memory of their abuse. Variables most predictive of abuse-related amnesia were sexual violence at an early age, extended abuse, and variables reflecting especially violent abuse (e.g., victimisation by multiple perpetrators, having been physically injured as a result of the abuse, victim fears of death if she or he disclosed the abuse to others). In contrast, abuse characteristics more likely to produce psychological conflict (e.g., enjoyment of the abuse, acceptance of bribes, feelings of guilt or shame) were not associated with abuse-related amnesia.

Real and delusional selves

Burman (2002) examines how those questioning the very project of psychotherapy propose that by exploring previously forgotten or dismissed material we create fictions out of the lived truths of people's lives. In working with patients with DID we are forced to deal with issues of belief, memory, and time on a daily basis. As Sinason has written: "At one level the idea that five different people could all have time-shares in one body seems absurd. And yet, it is both delusional and real and all at the same time" (2002, p. 7). We begin with the unavoidable dichotomy presented by the DID patient that he is more than one man. This may be seen as a triumph of the concrete over the symbolic, metaphorical splitting of the psyche as a defensive response to early trauma. And yet, for the patient, his lived experience is a truth that cannot be contradicted. Each self is real to the patient and has to be experienced and related to as real by the therapist. Early on in his work with me Eric questioned what the real aim of psychotherapy was. Was it to cure him of his sickness—to allow him to let go of the selves that had multiplied throughout his life and accept one core, un-splitable self? How possible was it to make a choice between integration and separateness? If integration is chosen then how possible will it be to attain what Sinason (2009) has described as "merger not murder"?

Despite the myriad ways in which his diagnosis had disabled his life, Eric was ambivalent about integrating his selves into one core self. He equated such a process with a form of murder, the killing-off of not just theoretical selves but actual people who have worked hard over the years to keep him alive. These fears were also voiced by the selves themselves; their terror of obliteration echoing Eric's fears of loss. I had to tread carefully through the course of therapy, knowing that my desire for Eric to become fully integrated, to become, in effect, a "normal" patient free from the clamour of his various competing selves, had to be secondary to Eric's real desire to continue to be dissociative. His condition caused him agonies: it triggered the implosion of numerous relationships, threatened his capacity to work, and compromised his physical health. Knowing this, it was some time before I realised that I had to recognise the limits of my own desire to rid him of his condition. While some symptom reduction did take place and allowed him some relief from the worst facets of his condition, I had to acknowledge that there was a profound attachment between most of Eric's selves. To seek to diminish or remove any of them would induce a murderous transference from which the therapy would not recover.

Working models

In his analysis of DID through the lens of attachment theory, Southgate (2002) lists four working models of DID patients:

1. The associating multiple person who, at the end of a successful therapy, is able to choose which self-states are appropriate at particular moments in time.
2. The repressed multiple person who "may seem singular rather than multiple" (p. 90), whose multiple selves are accessed primarily through dreams.
3. The dissociating multiple person with no psychotic selves, their key factor being that they blame themselves rather than the Other.
4. The dissociating multiple person with psychotic selves who rarely volunteers for therapy and can sometimes be an abuser.

Of these four groups, it is the last for whom the prognosis tends to be poorest. One should not, however, run away with the idea that the first three groups will not present clinical challenges for which our psychotherapeutic trainings can leave us ill-equipped. Maintaining the analytic frame is essential in all work with male survivors, but tends to come under the most severe strain when working with patients with DID. I tend, in these cases, to concur with Bass's (2007) perspective on the analytic frame as co-created and contextual, reflecting the variability of the psychoanalytic situation and the uniqueness of each dyad. The frame is solid, and secure, but will not always resemble the frame surrounding work with the worried well. Whatever pressures are placed upon it, however, it has to continue to symbolise a therapeutic structure with clear and safe boundaries. As Bass says, "the establishment of the frame is, at the same time, an integral part of the process itself and reflects conscious and unconscious aspects of both patient and analyst" (2007, p. 1).

Boundary pushing and breaking

There were times when Eric pushed the boundaries to breaking point. One self, "Georgie", an extremely needy, anxious part of him whose ego strength was tissue-thin, began to bring in gifts for me, positioned as symbols of gratitude for the help I was giving him and his fellow selves. The gifts grew incrementally, from cards, to books and CDs to, eventually, expensive items of clothing. The more I refused these gifts, the greater Georgie's sense of rejection became. My interpretations about the gifts were not quite rejected—it was more as if they had not even been made. I came to feel paralysed and persecuted by his ongoing attempts to make me accept his presents, eventually coming to feel as if I were depriving him by my attempts to keep to a boundary. "You hate me," Georgie would sigh, as yet another gift was refused. "You think I'm horrible, like everyone thinks I'm horrible."

It was through my work with groups that some solutions to this dilemma began to present themselves. In facilitating groups for male survivors I had made use of group analytic thinking to differentiate group processes from individual processes. For example, it had been helpful to interpret one group member's terror of opening up about his abuse as belonging to the group—he was articulating a profound emotion on behalf of the other men in the group. Such interpretations can relieve both the individual and the group from the paranoid fear that they have sole ownership of a particular thought or feeling. I began to interpret Georgie's gifts as an attempt by many of the selves to fend off their terror of loss: "Perhaps," I suggested, "you're working hard on behalf of everyone to let me know how scared you can be that you'll lose me. It may be hard to believe that if you didn't keep buying me presents I would still want to be here with you." Working with the complex interplay of selves presented by a DID patient can resemble working with a disruptive, unboundaried group who share little in common apart from their history of abuse. Add to this complexity the fact that the group includes children as well as adults, most members don't listen to others, and there may well be a different group of males from one session to the next.

Boundary infringements also occur outside the margins of sessions. Patients may, for example, telephone between appointments to report that one self is feeling suicidal. In seeking to kill one self the DID patient is not, of course, just contemplating suicide. The feeling and the act are also murderous. For this, amongst other reasons, I would struggle to work with a patient with DID in private practice. The one time I attempted to see a patient outside the confines of a specialist clinic the patient ended the work after a month of treatment. It was, I think, a wise decision. Some colleagues do this work within their private practice, and my feelings should not be read as a condemnation of them, rather than as an acknowledgement of my own fragility in this area. I feel too aware of the enormity of the trauma to feel I can conduct this work without a tight infrastructure of the kind provided by such specialists as the Clinic for Dissociative Studies in London. This has tended to include a support therapist, specialist supervisor, and access to psychiatric and legal consultancy when needed. The support therapist is necessary for more than just holiday cover, as some patients require daily treatment of an intensity that is too much for one psychotherapist to manage. As far as possible the differences between the two therapists are marked, one being the core therapist, the other the support therapist. Despite this demarcation of duties, it is inevitable that attempts to split the two in destructive ways are attempted by parts of the patient, necessitating strong clinical management to help prevent patient pathologies getting too forcibly projected into and between therapists.

The need for a collective response to the DID patient is not simply a healthy mirroring of the collective self presented by the patient. DID tends to have its roots in severe, cumulative trauma. The narratives presented by patients have a visceral, unnerving, and horrific impact upon the listener. We hear the most bizarre, bloodcurdling, agonising details of ritualised abuse, sadistic tortures, and murders of babies, transforming the consulting room from a place of quiet reflection to a scene from a horror movie. Attachments are not merely chaotic, they can also be infanticidal (Kahr, 2007a). Patients can switch from self to self with no warning, leaving the therapist in a state of hypervigilance much like that adopted by survivors of trauma. Many selves have little time for the niceties of psychotherapeutic etiquette. Interpretations can feel like abusive, penetrating attacks; the transference can itself become concretised, with the therapist filled with aggressive and punishing projections. Abuse of the severity experienced by DID patients tends to blunt the capacity for metaphor and symbolisation, meaning that the therapist taking a break is not *like* an abandonment, it *is* an abandonment. This level of intensity is too much for one person to hold, be they the patient or the therapist.

Believing in the delusional and the real

Working with male survivors with dissociative identity disorder involves encounters with the most distressing and unbelievable forms of sexual abuse. It evokes important questions about credibility and belief on two levels: how much we can believe the seemingly incredible stories our patients bring with them, and how possible it is to believe in the extraordinary way these stories have cracked the survivor's psyche into different pieces. For some the best we can do is believe that the delusional and the real can coexist. The concretised ways in which trauma has been responded to have involved the patient having to take a black and white view of the world as being either for or against him. This will be tested out in the patient/therapist dyad from the minute the patient first enters the consulting room. To map our way through this precarious clinical territory requires a set of maps—foremost among them an awareness of developmental stages and an understanding of group processes. Working with a patient with DID is often the nearest an individual psychotherapist will get to working with a group. The group is a rebellious, difficult one, made up of boys and men at various stages of social and emotional development, and at various levels of therapeutic engagement. Some are helpful allies in the therapeutic project, keen to work and open to transformation. Others personify what Nitsun (2002) called anti-group forces, resistant to change and keen to sabotage the potential for improvement.

A realistic view of what therapy can achieve with this particularly challenging subset of patients is essential. There will be some whose psychic structure has been so profoundly shattered by early abuse that very little from the therapeutic process can be introjected. There will, though, be others with enough glimmers of ego strength to ensure a therapeutic alliance between myriad selves and the therapist can be achieved and maintained. It is inevitable that working with this patient population will involve us in questions about boundary, as the men with whom we work have been subject to the most unimaginable forms of organised, sadistic, and potentially murderous forms of trauma. Once a body has been violated to this degree it is difficult for the survivor to fully understand the therapist's insistence on their own boundary. Fears of acting out, suicidality, and other real-life breaches of the frame are part of the fabric of this work, necessitating a robust organisational structure in which both patient and therapist can feel properly held. This work is not for the faint-hearted.

CHAPTER TEN

A crowded marriage: working with couples

"Barbara" was referred to me by the therapist working with her husband, "Ian". In order to protect Ian's confidentiality, his therapist was unable to give me much information about him, beyond the fact that he was a survivor of childhood paternal incest, and that the impact of this was having a profound effect upon Barbara. Barbara had agreed that she needed some form of therapy, and had stated her preference for a male therapist, saying that she felt "it would take a man to understand Ian."

In our first consultation I was struck immediately by something very tightly coiled within Barbara. She was in her early forties but looked older, with something grey and desiccated about her appearance. It was not difficult to see how living with her husband's trauma had sucked much of the life from her. She shook my hand, her grip stronger than I had expected, giving me a sense of something robust hidden beneath this appearance of fragility she carried with her. I explained who I was, and what the purpose of the session was, to give her a sense of how I might work with her, prior to her deciding whether she wished to proceed to long-term work. She said she understood, but then said her main worry was confidentiality. She was a teacher, she explained, and she knew all about how confidentiality worked. There had been a number of child protection issues she had dealt with at her school, and she had learnt that, while all professionals involved were drilled thoroughly in the need for utter confidentiality, it had never taken long for the details of each case to leak out amongst a wider group of people. She imagined that the world of psychotherapy was the same, that much was made of the boundaries of the work, but that in practice a similar leaking could occur. I explained, probably rather defensively, that I placed importance upon confidentiality, but perhaps any assurances I could give her would be diluted by her own, very personal experiences of secrets being betrayed. My use of the word "personal" came from a sense that the deep emotion colouring her words stemmed from far more than professional experiences. She agreed that "betrayal" was a good word to use in relation to her situation, and proceeded to tell me more about Ian.

They had known each other for nearly twenty years, and had married a decade ago. They had two children, both boys. Ian was also a teacher, although they had never worked together. They had had a close friendship from the beginning, with romance gradually seeming more possible as the years went by. She described him as a gentle man, someone who had helped make her feel safe. I wondered why safety was important to her, and she touched on some difficult childhood experiences with her father, but stressed that this was not what she had come here to talk about. Her sex life with Ian had been nonexistent for the past four years, and had fizzled into nothing shortly after he disclosed to her that he had experienced sexual abuse as a boy. He had been abused by his father over a period of ten years, the abuse finally stopping just before his sixteenth birthday. While being shocked at his disclosure, she felt she responded sensitively, unlike Ian's mother, who maintained a stance of denial that her husband had abused her child. Barbara encouraged Ian to seek help from an organisation specialising in working with male survivors, and his therapy began shortly afterwards.

In the past year Barbara had discovered that Ian had been trawling various internet sites, searching for anonymous sex with other women. When challenged on this, Ian stated that his therapist had given him permission to explore women other than her, in order to bring life back to his libido. He said that he still loved her, but could not imagine having sex with her again, thinking of her more as a sibling or friend rather than a lover. Perhaps the most wounding admission he made was that there were times when he thought of her as his mother. Barbara cried as she recalled this, and said that this was the hardest thing to cope with—his sexual rejection of her. Ian had later admitted to her that the permission allegedly granted by his therapist to have sex with other partners had not, in fact, been given, as he was still trying to work up courage to talk to her about his compulsive longings for anonymous sex. Barbara described life with Ian as like "walking through a minefield. He is on edge all the time—so I never know what to say, what might cause him to blow up. He's told me some things about the abuse, and yes, it was horrific. I can see that. But …" her voice trailed off. She looked at me disconsolately, as if suddenly defeated by the enormity of the gulf between her and her husband. "How on earth can I help him?" she asked, her voice cracking with emotion. "What can I do? I don't want to make him worse, or trigger him in any way. And sometimes I think about going, leaving, just getting out of it all. But then, the worst thing, I suppose, it's that I still love him—I still feel all this love for him, but none of it gets returned."

Barbara went on to talk about her two sons, and Ian's fears about getting too close to them. For some time he had exhibited phobic symptoms when around them, as if terrified of resuming the closeness that had previously been a mark of their relationship. As the session drew to a close, Barbara returned to the issue of confidentiality and her fears of the "secrets" of her marriage being known outside the family. "It would destroy me," she said as she prepared to leave the consulting room. "I know I need to come back—but I get so scared of people finding out about Ian. I feel so ashamed that I haven't been able to help him more, that he's had to get help, that he's been with other women." In the end Barbara agreed to return, and engaged in therapy for a number of years. The work was supremely challenging for her, as it involved not only looking at Ian's issues but also at her own. She began to dare to look at the abuse that had marked her own childhood, and the various unconscious reasons why she had found herself drawn to Ian, a fellow survivor. Ian himself began to gain more agency over his compulsions and they gradually found ways of rebuilding the trust and security that he had removed from their marriage. Despite Barbara's understandable initial mistrust of the therapeutic process, she and Ian found ways to ensure that their marriage did not become another victim of abuse.

* * *

As we have seen, there are some survivors whose experiences of trauma have caused a complete shutting down of relating. To interact with another evokes an unconscious terror that abuse will be re-enacted. The survivor defends against the agonising threat of relationship by entering an autistic bubble in which his normal needs for attachment, intimacy, and sex are sliced away. This occurs, however, in the minority of cases. We are social, attachment-seeking creatures, and the experience of having being sexually abused does not appear, on the whole, to diminish the need for strong, intimate relationships (Allen et al., 2001). It does, however, add a complicating and sometimes traumatising dimension to these relationships. One act of sexual abuse has many different victims. Partners, children, siblings, parents, and friends can all be as vulnerable to the legacy of sexual violation as the primary victim himself. The fact that we tend to think of this impact as being secondary serves to diminish the full weight of the trauma that can be loaded onto the partner of a survivor. The study of vicarious traumatisation (see Chapter Eight) has taught us much about the toxic impact upon clinicians of working with sexual abuse (Bell et al., 2003; Kadambi & Ennis, 2004; Canfield, 2005; VanDeusen & Way, 2006; Conrad, 2011; Figley, 2013) but has had little to say about the cumulative impact of living with a survivor. The debilitating impact upon us as clinicians of sexual trauma being confined to our working hours has been amply demonstrated—what, then, must the impact be of living alongside such trauma on a daily, lifelong basis?

Secondary traumatisation

In thinking of sexual abuse as impacting on primary and secondary victims, we need to be careful about the language we use. There are important differences between the terms "secondary victimisation" and "secondary traumatisation". Secondary victimisation refers to the process that occurs for (primary) victim/survivors when they disclose sexual assault and receive negative or inadequate responses from family, friends, or systems. Remer and Elliot equated this with a profound form of loss for the primary victim that requires a process of mourning (1988, p. 389). Secondary traumatisation refers to the effects of the sexual assault on people who were not the primary victim of the assault, but are nonetheless adversely affected by it, for example, non-perpetrator family members and intimate partners (Astbury, 2006).

Ninety per cent of victims of child sexual abuse within the UK are abused by someone known to them (Radford et al., 2011). The fact of sexual abuse being a largely relational phenomenon rather than something previous generations preferred to view as an external ("stranger danger") threat has enormous implications for how survivors deal with adult relationships. Sexual abuse is an assault on the capacity to form secure attachments, leaving the survivor prone to anxious, avoidant, ambivalent, or chaotic attachment patterns. In seeking therapy, a survivor is often coming on behalf of someone else, such is his ambivalence about attaining something reparative purely for himself. This has to be identified early on in treatment, as a displaced motivation for therapy has a profound impact upon the patient's motivation and ability to engage. There are cases where the survivor tends to regard himself as the secondary victim. He is seemingly content with his symptomology and is attached to his neuroses, phobias, and obsessions, while his partner is the one struggling to avoid being completely overwhelmed by them.

Chiasmal impact of abuse

Most research into the impact of sexual abuse upon a survivor's partner has focused on the survivor being female and the partner being male (Emm & McKenry, 1988; Firth, 1997; Nelson & Wampler, 2000; Wiersma, 2003). The particular impact of sexual abuse upon a gay or lesbian couple tends, therefore, to be missing from the literature. Partners of survivors have reported the specific impact of their partner's abuse upon them as including social isolation, a lack of confidence in responding to their partner's trauma, and a fear that abuse has contaminated all aspects of their relationship (Brittain & Merriam, 1988). Survivors report more current relationship problems than non-survivors, marry younger, are likely to be divorced, perceive their relationship to be of lesser quality than those of others, and reporte a significantly higher risk of maltreatment by their partner (Davis & Petretic-Jackson, 2000; DiLillo, 2001; Rumstein-McKean & Hunsley, 2001). Kishur and Figley (1987) spoke of the *chiasmal* effect of sexual abuse, illustrating its capacity to become a traumatogenic point of contact between two people—one the survivor, one their partner. It is important here to highlight rather more hopeful aspects of relationships affected by sexual abuse, as it has been shown that interpersonal relationships are potential moderators and mediators of the relationship between childhood sexual abuse and long-term distress (Runtz & Schallow, 1997; Whiffen et al., 1999).

Christiansen et al.'s (2012) study into secondary victims of rape is unusual in its inclusion of male survivor experiences. They concluded many respondents found it difficult to emotionally support the survivor of abuse, with the knowledge or disclosure of sexual abuse severely impairing their relationship. Their sample showed significant levels of traumatisation in the secondary victims, with approximately one quarter of the respondents suffering from post-traumatic stress syndrome. Feinauer, Callahan, and Hilton (1996) examined the relationship between a person's ability to adjust to an intimate relationship and the level of severity of their childhood abuse. Their study revealed that as the severity of abuse increased, the scores measuring the ability to adjust to intimate relationships decreased.

In analysing the impact of sexual abuse upon the partner of the survivor, Jacob and Veach (2005) stressed the need for male partners and female partners to be understood as distinct populations; the effects on and responses of female partners of victim/survivors being of a different quality to those for male partners. In their study of female partners of male survivors of child sexual abuse, the women they spoke to reported experiencing abuse, rape, and unwanted sexual attention from their partners. They also reported being blamed for their partners' anger. Most of the women believed that the abusive sexual behaviour of their male partners was an "acting out" of their childhood sexual abuse. The authors qualify these findings by speculating that the women who volunteered to participate in the study may have been partly motivated by a wish to disclose their experiences of violence at the hands of their partners. Jacob and Veach also found evidence of significant negative impact upon couple and family functioning with emotional reactions, coping strategies, communication patterns, and sexual functioning corresponding to the three components of Maltas and Shay's (1995) trauma contagion model (threatened beliefs, chronic stress, and re-enactment of aspects of child sexual abuse). While their results concerning threatened beliefs and chronic stress can be replicated to other populations, such as partners of war veterans, the re-enactment of aspects of child sexual abuse seems unique.

Impact of abuse upon sex

It is no surprise that sex between couples can be a casualty of sexual abuse. In a study of survivors of childhood abuse (Courtois, 1979) eighty per cent of those victims surveyed reported ongoing sexual problems in their adult relationships. The younger they were when they were abused, the more significant their adult relationship difficulties were. Perilloux et al. (2012) concluded that the areas of female survivors' lives most adversely impacted by sexual abuse and rape were self-esteem, sexual reputation, frequency of sex, desire to have sex, and self-perceived value as a potential partner. Maltz listed the most common sexual consequences of sexual abuse as being:

> avoiding, fearing, or lacking interest in sex; approaching sex as an obligation; experiencing negative feelings such as anger, disgust, or guilt with touch; having difficulty becoming aroused or feeling sensation; feeling emotionally distant or not present during sex; experiencing intrusive or disturbing sexual thoughts and images; engaging in compulsive or inappropriate sexual behaviours; experiencing difficulty establishing or maintaining an intimate relationship; experiencing vaginal pain or orgasmic difficulties (women); and experiencing erectile, ejaculatory, or orgasmic difficulties (men). (2002, p. 323)

This is backed up by Laumann et al.'s (1999) finding that male victims of childhood sexual abuse were more likely to experience erectile dysfunction, premature ejaculation, and low sexual desire.

The atrophy of sex in long-term relationships is by no means a phenomenon exclusively experienced by survivors of sexual abuse (Kahr, 2007b). It is, however, something that sexual trauma can exacerbate. Ian and Barbara had experienced a near-complete breakdown in emotional and sexual intimacy, which threatened to dissolve their relationship. It has been argued that in such cases the survivor experiences his spouse simultaneously as the perpetrator and as the mother who did not know of the abuse and who could not be told (Buttenheim & Levendosky, 1994). The suggested treatment strategy rests on interpreting the central role of re-enactment in the couple's relationship difficulties, giving meaning to the unconscious wall that had been erected between them.

Single and dual-trauma couples

A concept I have drawn from work with survivors of war trauma is that of "single-trauma" and "dual-trauma" couples. Single-trauma couples are those in which only one partner has experienced a history of trauma (Nelson et al., 2002). Dual-trauma couples are those in which "both partners have experienced a trauma, or multiple traumas, which continue to impact their individual and relationship functioning" (Balcom, 1996, p. 432). Nelson, Wangsgaard et al, describe the dynamics of single-trauma couples as including polarised emotional roles, secrecy surrounding the trauma, and parentification of the non-traumatised partner. In the dual-trauma couple there is a valency towards issues of power and control, competition between partners, external boundary ambiguity, survivor guilt, preoccupied-dismissing patterns, and minimising the effects of past-trauma experiences.

Assessment

Minuchin and Fishman, citing Arthur Koestler's term, call the couple in therapy the "holon" (1981, p. 13), suggesting that one patient is indivisible from the context (i.e., the partner). Therapists are encouraged by Miller and Sutherland (1999) to consider the involvement of the partner (and significant family members) in the therapeutic process. In order to ascertain what level of therapeutic work should be undertaken with the holon, an assessment has first to be made of the survivor's capacity to use therapy, followed by his partner's, and, finally, of the couple's therapeutic readiness. Couples work should only be undertaken if both the survivor and his partner have been given an opportunity to examine their capacity to share a therapeutic space. This should not be taken as a given. It is particularly important that an individual therapeutic process has been undertaken by the survivor. Without this, it is likely that re-traumatisation will occur in the couple work.

Another possibility to be guarded against is that the work will be inhibited by the survivor's desire to protect his partner from the impact of his trauma. This applies to both single-trauma and dual-trauma couples, although with the latter group particular care must be taken in both the assessment and treatment stages. A longer period of individual therapy is recommended for couples where complex trauma has been a feature of both of their lives. Psychotherapy may then be viewed through two lenses. As a treatment in and of itself, or as a preparation for couple work. We need to be as clear as we can be about this following an initial assessment, otherwise we will feed confusion in the couple's mind as to the purpose and function of their individual therapies.

Psychoeducation

Couple work is where more psycho-educative interventions can be practised. Compton and Follette (2002) suggest that educational input around such issues as dissociation, affect regulation, substance abuse, self-harm, and the development of communication skills can be particularly useful for survivors and partners to work on together. This form of input can also be managed in a group context, in which the isolation felt by couples may be assuaged by their working alongside other couples who have faced similar challenges to them. Another group model for consideration is where survivors have their own group and their partners another. These may be run as entirely separate entities or be linked, running alongside each other.

Nasim and Nadan (2013) propose a form of therapeutic "witnessing" in working with single-trauma couples. This is founded on the assumption that establishing the witnessing that was absent during the traumatic event in childhood can break traumatic re-enactments in adulthood. They suggest twofold witnessing: the couple's therapist witnesses the re-enactments of the trauma in the couple's relationship, and the survivor's partner witnesses the trauma's effect on the survivor's personal life and relationship. Twofold witnessing, they argue, can help break the cycle of traumatic re-enactment and help the survivor integrate the events of his life into a more coherent, continuous narrative. The partner's presence also facilitates acknowledgement of what happened to the survivor, and helps the survivor elaborate on his stories of resistance, survival, and strength.

The role of resilience

It is important that couple therapy does not privilege damage over resilience. An important set of questions to pose towards the beginning of the work is "What has kept you together? What positive factors in this relationship have enabled you to not be completely destroyed by abuse? What has bonded you so robustly, despite all these terrible challenges?" This will provide us with insight into not just the individual working models of both partners, but how the working model of the couple itself is constructed. We know from our work with individual survivors that the human spirit is extraordinary in its capacity to survive great trauma. The same is true of couples. What is often required from the therapist is help with recognising and magnifying those pockets of strength and resilience that lie submerged by the effects of cumulative trauma.

In working with couples we have to focus on the symbolic meaning of communication within and between the dyad. A survivor describing himself as irrevocably broken, a victim of abuse so profound it has rendered him unable to function in life, invites a number of responses. We may feel tremendous compassion and sympathy. We may admire his capacity to describe so vividly the impact of complex trauma. His partner may, however, feel disempowered, incapable of making any emotional demands upon him for fear of shattering his fragile psychic structure. The function of trauma and the way in which it is verbalised is an indicator of the couple's capacity to have a shared insight into what it is and what it has done to their relationship. The function of the therapist at moments such as this is to act as a translator, helping the couple to construct a shared language with which to conceptualise trauma and recovery. In dual-trauma couples another function is to guard against a competitive strain contaminating the relationship. This can arise from each partner feeling that his or her experience of trauma—the *traumatic load* (Kolassa et al., 2010)—is more or less profound than that of the other. It is seen most vividly when the competition is for who is more traumatised, but can be equally corrosive when one partner wishes to downgrade the severity of their own abuse in the service of making their partner feel less stigmatised or damaged.

Countertransference reactions

It has been argued that there is more potential for countertransference reactions in working with couples because the dyadic dynamic happens in front of the therapist (Gehlert et al., 2013), and also, because of the triangular dimension of the work, involves the therapist more directly. We have to take care not to be drawn into powerful splitting processes in which our feelings of identification with one patient rather than the other threaten to be experienced as a favouring of one and an abandonment of the other. Splitting is, of course, an ever present threat in the work, and operates on a continuum from specific responses stimulated by anxiety, to fundamental styles of relating marked by emotional reactivity, impaired problem-solving, and relationship instability (Siegel, 2008). Working with a couple presents an opportunity not just to observe the impact of trauma upon the relationship, but also allows the invaluable, if challenging, *experiencing* of the dynamics of the relationship as they are being played out. A particular challenge of this work is to analyse which dysfunctional elements of the couple's relationship stem from experiences of sexual abuse and which are part of the DNA of the couple's relationship, regardless of external trauma. It is rarely possible to cleanly divide between the two. Couples may have been drawn together because of their traumatic histories, or one may have gravitated towards the other in order to play the part of healer to the wounded (or, indeed, vice versa).

The ability to parent

Sexual abuse also impacts upon the survivor's and partner's experiences of being parents. Theoretical frameworks and empirical evidence suggest that an individual's developmental history, especially if it includes childhood sexual abuse, plays a significant role in the development of one's parenting skills (Kim et al., 2010; Berlin et al., 2011). Exposure to ongoing violence and abuse as a child has been shown to influence some people's capacity to exhibit requisite parenting skills if they have not received adequate and early ongoing support (van der Kolk et al., 1996; Banyard et al., 2003). Banyard (1997) concluded that survivors of sexual abuse were more susceptible to negative views of their parenting skills, particularly in the area of frequency of worry about child problems and how child discipline problems were handled. While most research highlights the adverse effects on survivors' parenting capabilities, it should be noted that it may also have beneficial consequences. While experiencing sexual abuse as a child may make a father paranoid about the potential sexual abuse of his child, it may have the positive effect of making the parent more empathetic to and strongly supportive of the child if sexual abuse is suspected or disclosed

(Hornor, 2010). Being a parent with a history of sexual abuse is bound to evoke paranoid anxieties about one's capacity to keep children safe, underpinning the need for therapy to provide a reality-testing dimension in which the strengths of the parental dyad can be looked at as much as the perceived weakness.

Shared relational histories

It is clear that as much care should be taken in assessing the needs of the couple as the needs of the individual. It is rare to find that the long-term aftermath of sexual abuse does not have a profound impact upon the partners of survivors, leaving them as vulnerable to trauma as the men they love. The capacity of the couple to respond to this trauma depends as much upon their shared relational history as it does upon their individual narratives. While this chapter has focused primarily upon the therapeutic needs of the couple, the needs of the wider family should also be taken into account. Male survivors may not just be partners, they may also be fathers, brothers, and sons. It is to be expected that each role will be impacted by sexual abuse, meaning that in assessing for individual therapeutic needs a parallel assessment as to wider family needs should be undertaken. As with so many aspects of trauma therapy, a purely individual approach may not be enough—a systemic perspective may be required to ensure that an individual pathology does not contaminate the whole family matrix.

CHAPTER ELEVEN

Becoming visible: on seeing and being seen

"Benjamin" enters the room looking stricken. I have been his supervisor for some years, and have rarely seen him looking anything other than confident. "I've done a terrible thing," he says. My heart sinks, and I wonder what boundary he has broken. He is usually such a thoughtful and fastidious clinician, and it is hard to imagine him making a dramatic misstep in his work. "I forgot Michael," he says, his voice a mixture of bewilderment and shame. "I completely forgot him. He turned up for his session and I was out. He left this most awful message on my phone, thinking he must have got the time wrong. But he hadn't. For some reason I just hadn't put him in the diary, and I was off picking up some dry cleaning. God, how on earth could I have forgotten Michael?"

Benjamin's forgetting of his patient is both extraordinary and understandable. "Michael" is in his mid-sixties, an accountant for a firm in the City who is, in fact, someone it is easy to overlook. He was referred to Benjamin by his GP following a period of depression. He had seen a cognitive behavioural therapist for three months but had found it did nothing to erase his underlying sense of sadness and despair. Fairly early on in his work with Benjamin he had disclosed the fact that, as a boy, he had been abused by his drama teacher. His parents had sent him to boarding school at the age of five, and it was shortly after starting at this school that the abuse began. Michael was one of many boys who were subject to nocturnal assaults by this teacher, and, many years later, some of the survivors brought a successful civil action against the school, the teacher having long since died. Michael had read about the action in the newspaper, but at no point did it occur to him to join his former friends in their action. He had always felt somewhat apart from others, both at school and throughout his professional life. He described himself as "self-sufficient", and seemed to exude a sense of pride in this, even when he described how little he felt that his wife or children knew him. Attachments were hard for him to build and sustain, and it was somewhat surprising to him and those around him that he had found a wife and that the marriage was, on the surface, a happy one.

Benjamin is a busy therapist, with lots of patients needing supervisory attention. He had presented Michael at the very beginning of their work together, but some months went by before I realised that I had heard nothing since. We remarked on our joint forgetting of him, something that made sense in the light of how he had been in his initial session. This was before he disclosed his history of abuse, and the overriding impression he left was of a man who did not quite know what he was in therapy for, with Benjamin feeling equally uncertain as to what it was that needed attention. He described his depression in a passive way; it was something that "came and went", nothing too dramatic, something he could, he felt, live with. His marriage was "OK", not too happy, not too unhappy. He barely mentioned his three children, and, until his disclosure, it was very easy to forget their existence completely. He even dressed in a forgettable way, his grey, nondescript clothes seeming to magnify his capacity to blend, unseen, into the background.

Over time Michael began to talk more about his early childhood. He described his parents as "good people who did their best", and sought to contextualise their sending him to boarding school in the social mores of the time. "That's what people of their class did. It was normal; it still is, in many ways." All of which was true but all of which missed the emotional point. Michael struggled to understand Benjamin's curiosity about how he had felt at the age of five when separated from his parents, and clung onto his emotionless narrative that it was intended to do him good, despite all that subsequently happened to him. It was in discussing the abuse that Michael finally allowed his defences to lower. He managed to describe the fear of hurt he had felt as the abuse continued, and the agonising sexual confusion it had left him with. A clue as to the elusive nature of Michael's internal world was presented when Benjamin sought to clarify the exact age Michael was when the abuse had stopped. Michael looked aghast at the question, and hesitated before answering. As soon as the words were out of his mouth Benjamin remembered asking exactly the same question, and eliciting the same answer, some sessions before. Michael was too polite to point out Benjamin's forgetfulness, but it clearly stung him, this confirmation of his sense of himself as someone who could be so easily lost and forgotten.

In dealing with Benjamin's actual forgetting of their appointment, we found ourselves recalling how difficult it had been in that first supervision presentation for Benjamin to answer me when I asked what Michael looked like. Even then there was something invisible about him. The dreadful re-enactment of Michael's parents allowing him to be separated from them at the age of five finally awakened Benjamin to the need to attend to his countertransferential amnesia. He was someone who could easily be sent away, whose early life experiences of separation and loss had created a transference template that had to be actively guarded against. Unless Benjamin worked harder at keeping Michael in mind, he would continue to be forgotten, both inside the consulting room and beyond.

* * *

It is worryingly easy for male survivors to vanish from view. They are in danger of occupying too liminal a place in the clinical world, our view of them diluted by the complex conflation of gender and sexual abuse. Because we struggle to think of men as victims of sexual abuse, we struggle to hold them in mind. This is especially true for men such as Michael who even before their experiences of sexual abuse have suffered the trauma of emotional deprivation and neglect. Despite its status as a socially sanctioned, normative experience for boys of a certain class, the impact of being sent to boarding school at an early age with the sudden and often irrevocable loss of their primary attachments constitutes a significant trauma. When sexual abuse by staff or other children follows, making new attachment figures unsafe, a defensive and protective encapsulation of the self may be acquired; the true identity of the person then remains hidden. This pattern distorts intimate relationships and continues into adult life (Schaverien, 2011, 2015).

Benjamin's forgetting of Michael represented a mirroring of his being put out of mind by his parents as much as by those within the school whose job was to keep him safe. Out of sight truly meant out of mind.

Attachment and mirroring

Being seen is irrevocably connected with attachment, the forging of an alliance in which trauma can be brought, understood, and processed. When we are faced with men who are hard to see we are also struggling with a core connection that has its roots in the interface between early deprivation and later abuse. Being seen involves being mirrored. Kohut (1971) emphasised the need for phase appropriate mirroring (from eighteen months to three years) in the development of a healthy narcissistic economy—the child that is the gleam in the mother's eye. Winnicott viewed the mirror as the loving gaze of the primary carer: "In individual emotional development the precursor of the mirror is the mother's face ... What does the baby see when he or she looks at the mother's face? I am suggesting that, ordinarily, what the baby sees is himself or herself" (Winnicott, 1967, p. 112). In his formulation of the concept of mirror phenomena Foulkes wrote of mirror reactions that are "characteristically brought out when a number of persons meet and interact. The person sees himself, or part of himself—often a repressed part of himself—reflected in the interactions of other group members. He sees them reacting in the way he does himself, or in contrast to his own behaviour. He also gets to know himself—and this is a fundamental process in ego development—by the effect he has on others and the picture they form of him" (Foulkes, 1964, p. 110). Pines (1984) links mirror reactions to therapeutic processes and early developmental processes, recalling Foulkes and Anthony's (1965) description of the child's emergence from narcissism through the greater awareness of the self, evoked by reflection coming from outside, which helps him to differentiate between what he is and what he is not.

Pines also highlights Buss's (1980) finding that:

> the very presence of a mirror in a room has a distinct psychological effect ... the person is both more self-aware of the internal world, its values and standards, and makes more effort to live up to them even though they do not look into the mirror. The presence or absence of a mirror in the experimental set-up has been shown

> to affect a person's ability to resist suggestion and to withstand pressures to betray their principles, for instance to inflict pain on others in experiments, when they are opposed to such behaviour. Seeing oneself on video tapes, however, has the opposite effect for one is then more likely to conform to social norms and to respond to group pressures ... The mirror effect, therefore, helps us to preserve our individuality in the face of external pressures. (Pines, 1984, p. 28)

Eye contact

Eye contact both decodes and encodes communication. It is an immensely intimate form of interaction and implies the creative of an intersubjectivity, a real "seeing eye to eye." The emotional meaning of two pairs of eyes meeting is also influenced by cultural factors. In Western cultures maintaining eye contact implies an interest in the person you are looking at and what that person is saying. Poor eye contact implies a lack of interest in the other or a lack of confidence in oneself. Within Europe it can also be dependent on location. In the UK public transport is a place where eye contact is avoided; we hide our gaze and that of others behind newspapers, Kindles, and smartphones. In other European countries eye contact in public places is less inhibited. Middle Eastern cultures, largely Muslim, have strict rules regarding eye contact between the sexes. Intense eye contact between those of the same gender—especially between men—can be a signifier of credibility; the returning of the gaze communicating trust and belief. In many Asian, African, and Latin American cultures, extended eye contact can be taken as an affront or a challenge of authority.

We have to think about the ways in which we look at and see our patients. We are familiar with the feminist notion of the gendered gaze, in which women are objectified by the male lens through which they are viewed (Schaverien, 2003) but less aware of the impact of the therapeutic gaze upon the male survivor. Our awareness of the primacy of the capacity to be seen by the mother and the beautiful reciprocity of eye contact between healthy infant and healthy mother needs to be accompanied by an awareness of the complex abused/abuser transference associations that the gaze also evokes. Seeing and being seen are not always natural processes for therapist or patient. It should be remembered that Freud himself disliked being constantly looked at by his patients and this, amongst other considerations, led him to construct the situation of the patient on the couch with the analyst sitting behind him. Being seen for some patients is too closely and intimately connected with the experience of being viewed as a sexual object. Laing used the term "petrification" to describe the state of paralysis that some people experiencing psychosis enter into when they are caught in the gaze of others: "In psychotic conditions the gaze and scrutiny of the other can be experienced as an actual penetration to the core of the 'inner self'" (1960, p. 106). A similar paralysis can occur when the transference too closely echoes the abused/abuser dynamic.

Invisibility in the transference

Davies and Frawley (1994) delineated four transference/countertransference paradigms that emerge when working with survivors of sexual abuse:

i. sadistic victimiser relating to an angry but helpless victim;
ii. collaborator in a seductive relationship;
iii. powerful but idealised rescuer;
iv. non-abusive but neglectful parent.

They all have in common a relation with how the patient feels he is seen, with the fourth paradigm coming closest to that enacted in much of our work with male survivors—the survivor as the child whose pain is never seen, the invisible boy who becomes the invisible man. In the transference we come to represent the parental figure who was either blind to the abuse or *turned a blind eye* in a more worrying, collusive way. We also symbolise the society that cannot bear to look at abuse inflicted on boys and men, preferring to maintain an illusory split between the powerful, invulnerable male, and the weak, fragile female. Acting as a form of mirror for our patients may relieve some of them from the agony of what they see when they look at themselves. The anorexic who only sees obesity, the gender dysphoric who cannot bear to focus on one gender or another, or the forensic patient who cannot see beyond a pervasive identification with his aggressor all need to meet a contemplative gaze that can mirror something less distorted by trauma.

Many survivors of abuse will have tried to make themselves invisible—either as a boy desperately trying to escape the objectifying, violent gaze of his abusers, or as a man seeking to erase any shaming signs of assault and rape from the sight of others. This will have resulted in a core difficulty in claiming one's place in the world. When one's sense of self has been atrophied by trauma (the singular trauma of abuse or the cumulate traumata of abuse, neglect, and deprivation) it is difficult to feel one has a place in the world, and that one can be seen through anything other than a lens of perversion and hurt.

Overidentification with the invisible

Benjamin's work with Michael ultimately benefited from his forgetting of the session, as it enabled them both to finally look at the invisible dynamic within their work together. In the session following the forgotten one Michael insisted that he had not been affected by Benjamin's absence—"These things happen," he said. "That's life. It's not as if anyone was killed." Benjamin refused to collude with Michael's need to minimise the tremendous wound he felt at having been forgotten once more and, in doing so, found himself feeling more alive and potent in the work. A complex process of overidentification with Michael's invisibility had taken place from the first session. As a response to Michael's passivity and compliance, Benjamin had seemed to dim down his own presence in their work. Normally a vital, assertive, and enlivened clinician, Benjamin had found himself being muted by Michael's quietness, mistaking an appropriate level of gentle sensitivity for what was more of an absence. He and Michael had become enmeshed in an unspoken alliance of passivity in which vitality had been suppressed and killed off.

In addressing this in Benjamin's supervision I found myself drawing on Anne Alvarez's work with autistic patients who presented with deadness of affect, as mentioned in Chapter Eight. Alvarez (2012) writes about a level of analytic work that seeks to vitalise the deadened state of mind. This stands apart from the two other levels she has identified as being explanatory/locating or descriptive/naming interpretations—levels of interpretation that fit more neatly into a classic notion of analytic neutrality. What Alvarez is describing is a form of interpretation that recognises the need for something more enlivening, something that acknowledges the atrophied and deadened aspects of a patient's psyche, and that seeks not only to wake these parts up, but which also reminds the patient that the therapist has not been killed off by his very deadened state. The therapist is interested enough to want to bring something to life. Through this process the therapist becomes more visible to the patient and, following on from this, the patient becomes more visible to the therapist.

In working effectively with Benjamin I also had to attend to how and why Michael had become invisible to *me*. I had become a secondary victim of invisibility, and had to struggle, just as my supervisee had to, with holding Michael in mind. In reflecting upon this in my own supervision, I came to reflect on the cumulative nature of trauma in psychotherapy with male survivors. I had myself been impacted by various different layers of trauma; the pain of Michael's object-relational history—shaped by his neglectful and abandoning parents—and the appalling violation of his sexual abuse had combined with something deeply rooted in Michael's pathology to throw a cloak of invisibility over all three of us. He was someone it was too easy and too seductive to ignore and forget. Our collective amnesia was a vivid enactment of the lack of healthy mirroring in his early life and the later exacerbation of this in how his abuser had exploited a potentially healthy relationship and yearned-for attachment. Michael's invisibility was formed by more than one trauma and had become fused in a powerful projective enactment.

The lacuna of male abuse

This book was written in response to a lacuna. Unless something is described it cannot be understood. I have used men's stories to illustrate various theories and ideas because I think stories are the best way of making the theoretical real. But another reason for the use of stories was my frustration at the narratives of male survivors so rarely featuring in our collective accounts of psychotherapy and counselling. The absence of such stories from our textbooks could be indicative of a lack of male survivors entering the consulting room. And yet I doubt it. In speaking with colleagues about their practices I have been struck by how many male survivors have, in fact, been seen for individual and group psychotherapy over the years. It seems to be the case that men's experiences of sexual abuse are not identified by them as their primary reason for seeking therapeutic help. Instead they come for help with depression, self-harm, relationship problems, eating disorders, and other compulsions. Some have gone through long periods of therapy without ever having disclosed their abusive histories—a shameful indictment of an aversion to working with the cause as well as the symptom.

It is my hope that in raising our awareness of the prevalence of male sexual abuse, the invisibility of these men can be illuminated. I also hope that the various stories recounted here can contribute to a greater understanding of the suitability of psychotherapy as an effective treatment for the long-lasting, complex, and debilitating after-effects of sexual trauma. It is curious to discover an area of human experience where men are treated less equally than women, and where the implicit perception of male power actually serves to disempower. In examining the therapeutic needs of male survivors I hope that my findings are of relevance not only in how we think about and treat male victims of sexual abuse, but more broadly in how we consider the place of the male in the consulting room.

REFERENCES

Abelove, H. (1986). Freud, male homosexuality, and the Americans. In: H. Abelove, M. Barale, & D. Halperin (Eds), The Lesbian and Gay Studies Reader (pp. 381–393). New York: Routledge.

Alexander, P. C. (1992). "Application of attachment theory to the study of sexual abuse." *Journal of Consulting and Clinical Psychology*, *60*(2): 185–195.

Allen, J. G., Huntoon, J., Fultz, J., Stein, H., Fonagy, P., & Evans, R. B. (2001). "A model for brief assessment of attachment and its application to women in inpatient treatment for trauma-related psychiatric disorders." *Journal of Personality Assessment*, *76*(3): 421–447.

Allnock, D., & Miller, P. (2013). *No One Noticed, No One Heard: A Study of Disclosures of Childhood Abuse*. London, NSPCC.

Alvarez, A. (1992). *Live Company: Psychoanalytic Psychotherapy with Autistic, Borderline, Deprived and Abused Children*. London: Routledge.

Alvarez, A. (2012). *The Thinking Heart: Three Levels of Psychoanalytic Therapy with Disturbed Children*. London: Routledge.

Anda, R. F., Felitti, V. J., Bremner, J. D., Walker, J. D., Whitfield, C., Perry, B. D., Dube, S. R., & Giles, W. H. (2006). "The enduring effects of abuse and related adverse experiences in childhood." *European Archives of Psychiatry and Clinical Neuroscience*, *256*(3): 174–186.

Anderson, A., Cohn, L., & Holbrook, T. (2000). Making Weight: Men's Conflicts With Food Weight, Shape and Appearance. Carlsbad, CA: Gurze.

Astbury, J. (2006). *Services for Victim/Survivors of Sexual Assault: Identifying Needs, Interventions and Provision of Services in Australia*. Melbourne: Australian Centre for the Study of Sexual Assault, Australian Institute of Family Studies.

Auerbach, W. (2014). "Time and timelessness in the psychoanalysis of an adult with severe childhood trauma." *Studies in Gender and Sexuality, 15*(3): 199–213.

Bach, S. (1977). "On the narcissistic state of consciousness." *International Journal of Psychoanalysis, 58*: 209–233.

Balcom, D. (1996). "The interpersonal dynamics and treatment of dual trauma couples." *Journal of Marital and Family Therapy, 22*(4): 431–442.

Balint, M. (1979). *The Basic Fault: Therapeutic Aspects of Regression*. Evanston, IL: Northwestern University Press.

Banyard, V. L. (1997). "The impact of childhood sexual abuse and family functioning on four dimensions of women"s later parenting." *Child Abuse & Neglect, 21*: 1095–1107.

Banyard, V. L., Williams, L. M., & Siegel, J. A. (2003). "The impact of complex trauma and depression on parenting: An exploration of mediating risk and protective factors." *Child Maltreatment, 8*: 334–349.

Bass, A. (2007). "When the frame doesn"t fit the picture." *Psychoanalytic Dialogues, 17*(1): 1–27.

Bassiouni, M., & McCormick, M. (1996). Sexual violence: An invisible weapon of war in the former Yugoslavia. *Journal of the American Medical Association, 304*: 553–562.

Batten, S. V., Follette, V. M., & Aban, I. B. (2002). Experiential avoidance and high-risk sexual behavior in survivors of child sexual abuse. *Journal of Child Sexual Abuse, 10*: 101–120.

Bebbington, P. E., Cooper, C., Minot, S., Brugha, T. S., Jenkins, R., Meltzer, H., & Dennis, M. (2009). Suicide attempts, gender, and sexual abuse: Data from the 2000 British Psychiatric Morbidity Survey. *American Journal of Psychiatry, 166*: 1135–1140.

Becker, E. (1997). *The Denial of Death*. New York: Free.

Bell, H., Kulkarni, S., & Dalton, L. (2003). Organizational prevention of vicarious trauma. *Families in Society: The Journal of Contemporary Social Services, 84*: 463–470.

Bell, S. T., Kuriloff, P. J., & Lottes, I. (1994). Understanding attributions of blame in stranger rape and date rape situations: An examination of gender, race, identification, and students' social perceptions of rape victims. *Journal of Applied Social Psychology, 24*: 1719–1734.

Belsky, J. (1993). Etiology of child maltreatment: A developmental ecological analysis. *Psychological Bulletin, 114*: 413–434.

Bender, L., & Blau, A. (1937). The reaction of children to sexual relations with adults. *American Journal of Orthopsychiatry, 7*: 500–518.

Benjamin, J. (1996). *Like Subjects, Love Objects: Essays on Recognition and Sexual Difference*. New Haven, CT: Yale University Press.

Berlin, L. J., Appleyard, K., & Dodge, K. A. (2011). Intergenerational continuity in child maltreatment: Mediating mechanisms and implications for prevention. *Child Development, 82*: 162–176.

Bick, E. (1968). The experience of the skin in early object-relations. *International Journal of Psychoanalysis, 49*: 484–486.

Bieber, I., Dain, H., Dince, P., Drellich, M., Grand, H., Gundlach, R., Kremer, M., Rifkin, A., Wilbur, C., & Bieber, T. (1962). *Homosexuality: A Psychoanalytic Study*. New York: Basic.

Bifulco, A., Brown, G. W., & Adler, Z. (1991). Early sexual abuse and clinical depression in adult life. *The British Journal of Psychiatry, 159*: 115–122.

Blechner, M. J. (1998). Maleness and masculinity. *Contemporary Psychoanalysis, 34*: 597–613.

Bliss, E. L. (1986). *Multiple personality, allied disorders, and hypnosis*. Oxford: Oxford University Press.

Bollas, C. (1989). *Forces of Destiny: Psychoanalysis and Human Idiom*. London: Free Association.

Bonime, W. (1982). Psychotherapy of the depressed patient. *Contemporary Psychoanalysis, 18*: 173–189.

Bourke, J. (2014). Shell Shock and the Shock of Shells: World War One: The War that Changed the World [radio programme]. Broadcast on Radio 3, 31 december 2014.

Bourne, A., Reid, D., Hickson, F., Torres Rueda, S., & Weatherburn, P. (2014). *The Chemsex Study: Drug Use in Sexual Settings Among Gay and Bisexual Men in Lambeth, Southwark and Lewisham*. London: Sigma Research, and London School of Hygiene and Tropical Medicine.

Bowen, E. (1975). Notes on writing a novel. In: S. Brown (Ed.), *Pictures and Conversations: Chapters of an autobiography, with other collected writings* (pp. 167–193). New York: Alfred A. Knopf.

Bowlby, J. (1980). *Attachment and Loss, Volume 3: Loss: Sadness and Depression*. London: International Psychoanalytical Library.

Bradford, J., Reisner, S. L., Honnold, J. A., & Xavier, J. (2013). Experiences of transgender-related discrimination and implications for health: Results from the Virginia Transgender Health Initiative Study. *American Journal of Public Health, 103*: 1820–1829.

Brady, J. L., Guy, J. D., Poelstra, P. L., & Brokaw, B. F. (1999). Vicarious traumatization, spirituality, and the treatment of sexual abuse survivors: A national survey of women psychotherapists. *Professional Psychology: Research and Practice, 30*: 386–393.

Braun, B. G. (1989). Psychotherapy of the survivor of incest with a dissociative disorder. *Psychiatric Clinics of North America, 12*: 307–324.

Briere, J., & Conte, J. (1993). Self-reported amnesia for abuse in adults molested as children. *Journal of traumatic stress, 6*(1): 21–31.

Briere, J., & Elliott, D. M. (2003). Prevalence and psychological sequelae of self-reported childhood physical and sexual abuse in a general population sample of men and women. *Child Abuse and Neglect, 27*: 1205–1222.

Brittain, D. E., & Merriam, K. (1988). Groups for significant others of survivors of child sexual abuse: A report of methods and findings. *Journal of Interpersonal Violence, 3*: 90–101.

Bromberg, P. (2006). *Awakening the Dreamer: Clinical Journeys*. New Jersey: Analytic.

Bromberg, P. M. (1983). The mirror and the mask: On narcissism and psychoanalytic growth. *Contemporary Psychoanalysis, 19*: 359–387.

Brothers, D. (2014). Traumatic attachments: Intergenerational trauma, dissociation, and the analytic relationship. *International Journal of Psychoanalytic Self Psychology, 9*(1): 3–15.

Brown, J. M., Hamilton, C., & O'Neill, D. (2007). Characteristics associated with rape attrition and the role played by scepticism or legal rationality by investigators and prosecutors. *Psychology, Crime and Law, 13*: 355–370.

Brownmiller, S. (1975). *Against Our Will: Men, Women and Rape*. London: Martin Secker & Warburg.

Burman, E. (2002). Therapy as memory-work: Dilemmas of discovery, recovery and construction. *British Journal of Psychotherapy, 18*: 457–469.

Buss, A. H. (1980). *Self Consciousness and Social Anxiety*. London: W. H. Freeman.

Buttenheim, M., & Levendosky, A. (1994). Couples treatment for incest survivors. *Psychotherapy: Theory, Research, Practice, Training, 31*: 407–414.

Byne, W., Bradley, S. J., Coleman, E., Eyler, A. E., Green, R., Menvielle, E. J., Meyer-Bahlburg, H. F., Pleak, R. R., & Tompkins, D. A. (2012). Report of the American Psychiatric Association task force on treatment of gender identity disorder. *Archives of Sexual Behavior*, 41: 759–796.

Cafri, G., Yamamiya, Y. Brannick, M., & Thompson, J. K. (2005). The influence of sociocultural factors on body image: A meta-analysis. *Clinical Psychology: Science and Practice, 12*: 421–433.

Canfield, J. (2005). Secondary traumatization, burnout, and vicarious traumatization. *Smith College Studies in Social Work, 75*: 81–101.

Carlat, D. J., Camargo, C. A., & Herzog, D. B. (1997). Eating disorders in males: A report on 135 patients. *American Journal of Psychiatry, 154*: 1127–1132.

Carmen, E., Rieker, P., & Mills, T. (1984). Victims of violence and psychiatric illness. In: P. Rieker & E. Carmen (Eds), *The Gender Gap in Psychotherapy* (pp. 199–211). New York: Springer.

Carnes, P. (1983). *Out of the Shadows: Understanding Sexual Addiction.* Minneapolis, MN: CompCare Publishers.

Carnes, P. J., Murray, R. E., & Charpentier, L. (2005). Bargains with chaos: Sex addicts and addiction interaction disorder. *Sexual Addiction and Compulsivity, 12*: 79–120.

Carr, R. (2002). Stigmas, gender and coping: A study of HIV+ Jamaicans. *Race, Gender and Class, 9*: 122–144.

Cashmore, J., & Shackel, R. (2013). The Long-term Effects of Child Sexual Abuse. Sydney: Australian Institute of Family Studies.

Cawson, P., Wattam, C., Brooker, S. & Kelly, G. (2000). *Child Maltreatment in the United Kingdom: A Study of the Prevalence of Abuse and Neglect.* London: NSPCC.

Christiansen, D., Bak, R. & Elklit, A. (2012). Secondary victims of rape. *Violence and Victims, 27*: 246–262.

Chu, J. A. (2008). Ten traps for therapists in the treatment of trauma survivors. In: C. Jacob and G. Adshead (Eds), *Personality Disorder: The Definitive Reader* (pp. 210–228). London: Jessica Kingsley.

Clements, H., Dawson, D. L, & das Nair, R. (2014). Female-perpetrated sexual abuse: a review of victim and professional perspectives. *Journal of Sexual Aggression, 20*: 197–215.

Cohn, L. (2013). *Male Gender Roles and Other Sociocultural Factors in Navigating Access to Treatment.* Paper presented at International Conference on Eating Disorders, 1–5 May 2013. Montreal, Canada.

Cole, G. W. (2001). Two cases of psychoanalytic psychotherapy with people with HIV/AIDS: Commentary on papers by Leli and Weinstein. *Journal of Gay and Lesbian Psychotherapy, 5*(2): 29–41.

Coleman, E. (1992). Is your patient suffering from compulsive sexual behavior? *Psychiatric Annals, 22*: 320–325.

Coleman, J. (2002). Dissociative disroders: Recognition within psychiatry and RAINS. In: V. Sinason (Ed.), *Attachment, Trauma and Multiplicity: Working with Dissociative Identity Disorder* (pp. 197–201). East Sussex: Routledge.

Compton, J. S., & Follette, V. M. (2002). Couple therapy when a partner has a history of child sexual abuse. In: N. S. Jacobson & A. S. Gurman (Eds), *Clinical Handbook of Couple Therapy* (pp. 466–486). New York: Guilford.

Conrad, D. (2011). Secondary trauma and caring professionals: Understanding its impact and taking steps to protect yourself. *The Link, 20*(2): 1–5.

Corbett, A. (2009). Words as a second language: The psychotherapeutic challenge of severe disability. In: T. Cottis (Ed.), *Intellectual Disability, Trauma and Psychotherapy* (pp. 45–62). London: Routledge.

Corbett, A. (2011). Silk purses and sows' ears: The social and clinical exclusion of people with intellectual disabilities. *Psychodynamic Practice, 17*: 273–289.

Corbett, A. (2014). *Disabling Perversions: Forensic Psychotherapy with People with Intellectual Disabilities*. London: Karnac.

Courtois, C. (1979). The incest experience and its aftermath. *Victimology: An International Journal, 4*: 337–347.

Cox, D. (2015). Are more men getting eating disorders?. *The Guardian*. Available at: www.theguardian.com/lifeandstyle/2015/jan/18/are-more-men-getting-eating-disorders (accessed April 2016).

Craparo, G. (2011). Internet addiction, dissociation, and alexithymia. *Procedia-Social and Behavioral Sciences, 30*: 1051–1056.

Craparo, G. (2014). The role of dissociation, affect dysregulation and developmental trauma in sexual addiction. *Clinical Neuropsychiatry, 11*: 86–90.

Crome, S. A. (2006). *Male Survivors of Sexual Assault and Rape*. Melbourne: Australian Institute of Family Studies.

Crowder, A. (1995). *Opening The Door: A Treatment Model for Therapy with Male Survivors of Sexual Abuse*. New York: Brunner/Mazel.

Cunningham, J., Pearce, T., & Pearce, P. (1988). Childhood sexual abuse and medical complaints in adult women. *Journal of Interpersonal Violence, 3*: 131–144.

Currin, L., Schmidt, U., Treasure, J., & Jick, H. (2005). Time trends in eating disorder incidence. *The British Journal of Psychiatry, 186*: 132–135.

Danner, M. (2004). *The Logic of Torture*. New York: New York Review of Books.

Davies, D. (2014). *In Plain Sight: The Life and Lies of Jimmy Savile*. London: Hachette.

Davies, J. M., & Frawley, M. G. (1994). *Treating the Adult Survivor of Childhood Sexual Abuse: A psychoanalytic perspective*. New York: Basic.

Davis, J. L., & Petretic-Jackson, P. A. (2000). The impact of child sexual abuse on adult interpersonal functioning: A review and synthesis of the empirical literature. *Aggression and Violent Behavior*, 5: 291–328.

DCSF (Department for Children, Schools and Families) (2010). Working Together to Safeguard Children Consultation Document: A guide to inter-agency working to safeguard and promote the welfare of children. Nottingham: DCSF.

DelZotto, A., & Jones, A. (2002). Male-on-Male Sexual Violence in Wartime: Human Rights' Last Taboo? Available at: http://adamjones.freeservers.com/malerape.htm (accessed April 2016).

DeMause, L. (1974). *The History of Childhood*. London: Methuen.

Denov, M. S. (2004). The long-term effects of child sexual abuse by female perpetrators: A qualitative study of male and female victims. *Journal of Interpersonal Violence, 19*: 1137–1156.

DiLillo, D. (2001). Interpersonal functioning among women reporting a history of childhood sexual abuse: Empirical findings and methodological issues. *Clinical Psychology Review, 21*: 553–576.

Dimen, M. (1991). Deconstructing difference: Gender, splitting, and transitional space. *Psychoanalytic Dialogues, 1*(3): 335–352.

Diseth, T. H. (2005). Dissociation in children and adolescents as reaction to trauma: An overview of conceptual issues and neurobiological factors. *Nordic Journal of Psychiatry, 59*: 79–91.

Doctor, R. (2003). *Dangerous Patients: A Psychodynamic Approach to Risk Assessment and Management*. London: Karnac.

Dorahy, M. J., & Clearwater, K. (2012). Shame and guilt in men exposed to childhood sexual abuse: A qualitative investigation. *Journal of Child Sexual Abuse, 21*: 155–175.

Eagly, A. H., Beall, A. E., & Sternberg, R. J. (2004). *The Psychology of Gender*. New York: Guilford.

Edelson, M. G. (2013). Why have all the boys gone? Gender differences in prosecution acceptance of child sexual abuse cases. *Sexual Abuse: A Journal of Research and Treatment, 25*: 461–481.

Edelson, M. G., & Joa, D. (2010). Differences in legal outcomes for male and female children who have been sexually abused. *Sexual Abuse: A Journal of Research and Treatment, 22*: 427–442.

Elise, D. (2001). Unlawful entry: Male fears of psychic penetration. *Psychoanalytic Dialogues, 11*: 499–531.

Elmone, P., Lingg, M., & Schwartz, M. F. (1996). Adult survivors of sexual trauma: A conceptualization for treatment. *Journal of Mental Health Counseling, 18*: 108–122.

Emm, D., & McKenry, P. C. (1988). Coping with victimization: The impact of rape on female survivors, male significant others, and parents. *Contemporary Family Therapy, 10*: 272–279.

Estellon, V., & Mouras, H. (2012). Sexual addiction: Insights from psychoanalysis and functional neuroimaging. *Socioaffective Neuroscience and Psychology*, 2. Available at: www.socioaffectiveneuroscipsychol.net/index.php/snp/article/view/11814 (accessed April 2016).

Eubanks, J. R., Kenkel, M. Y., & Gardner, R. M. (2006). Body-size perception, bodyesteem, and parenting history in college women reporting a history of child abuse. *Perceptual and Motor Skills, 102*: 485–497.

Fairburn, C. G., & Harrison, P. J. (2003). Eating disorders. *The Lancet, 361*: 407–416.

Feinauer, L. L., Callahan, E. H., & Hilton, H. G. (1996). Positive intimate relationships decrease depression in sexually abused women. *American Journal of Family Therapy, 24*: 99–106.

Feldman, M. B., & Meyer, I. H. (2007). Eating disorders in diverse lesbian, gay, and bisexual populations. *International Journal of Eating Disorders, 40*: 218–226.

Feltman, K. A., & Ferraro, F. R. (2011). Preliminary data on risk factors and disordered eating in male college students. *Current Psychology, 30*: 194–202.

Ferenczi, S. (1949). Confusion of the tongues between the adults and the child (the language of tenderness and of passion). *International Journal of Psychoanalysis, 30*: 225–230.

Fergusson, D. M., & Woodward, L. J. (2002). Mental health, educational, and social role outcomes of adolescents with depression. *Archives of General Psychiatry, 59*: 225–231.

Figley, C. R. (2013). *Compassion Fatigue: Coping with Secondary Traumatic Stress Disorder in Those Who Treat the Traumatized*. New York: Taylor & Francis.

Finkelhor, D. (1994). Current information on the scope and nature of child sexual abuse. *The Future of Children, 4*(2): 31–53.

Finney, A., & Britain, G. (2006). *Domestic Violence, Sexual Assault and Stalking: Findings from the 2004/05 British Crime Survey*. London: Home Office.

Firth, M. T. (1997). Male partners of female victims of child sexual abuse: Treatment issues and approaches. *Sexual and Marital Therapy, 12*(2): 159–171.

Follette, V. M., Polusny, M. M., & Milbeck, K. (1994). Mental health and law enforcement professionals: Trauma history, psychological symptoms, and impact of providing services to child sexual abuse survivors. *Professional Psychology: Research and Practice, 25*: 275–282.

Fordham, M. (1960). Counter-transference. *British Journal of Medical Psychology, 33*(1): 1–8.

Foster, T. A. (2011). The sexual abuse of black men under American slavery. *Journal of the History of Sexuality, 20*: 445–464.

Foulkes, S. H. (1964). Therapeutic Group Analysis. London, George Allen & Unwin.

Foulkes, S. H., & Anthony, E. J. (1965). *Group Psychotherapy: The Psychoanalytic Approach*. London: Penguin.

Freeman, A. C. (2005). Eating disorders in males: A review. *South African Journal of Psychiatry, 8*(2): 58–64.

Freud, A. (1936). *The Ego and the Mechanisms of Defence*. London: Hogarth.

Freud, S. (1905d). Three essays on the theory of sexuality. *S.E., 7*: 123–246. London: Hogarth.

Freud, S. (1910a). Five lectures on psycho-analysis. *S.E., 11*: 1–249. London: Hogarth.

Freud, S. (1910c). *Leonardo da Vinci and a Memory of His Childhood. S.E., 11*: 59–138. London: Hogarth Press.

Freud, S. (1914g). Remembering, repeating and working-through (further recommendations on the technique of psycho-analysis II). *S.E., 12*: 147–156. London: Hogarth.

Freud, S. (1917e). Mourning and melancholia. *S.E., 14*: 239. London: Hogarth.

Freud, S. (1920g). *Beyond the Pleasure Principle. S.E., 18*: 7. London: Hogarth.

Gardner, F. (1999). Transgenerational processes and the trauma of sexual abuse. *The European Journal of Psychotherapy, Counselling and Health, 2*: 297–308.

Gartner, R. (1999). *Betrayed as Boys: Psychodynamic Treatment of Sexually Abused Men*. New York: Guilford.

Gartner, R. B. (2014). Trauma and countertrauma, resilience and counterresilience. *Contemporary Psychoanalysis, 50*(4): 609–626.

Gavin, H. (2013). *Criminological and Forensic Psychology*. London: Sage.

Gedo, J. E. (1977). Notes on the psychoanalytic management of archaic transferences. *Journal of the American Psychoanalytic Association, 25*: 787–803.

Gehlert, K. M., Pinke, J., & Segal, R. (2013). A trainee's guide to conceptualizing countertransference in marriage and family therapy supervision. *The Family Journal, 22*(1): 7–16.

Gil, S. (2014). Male victims of childhood sexual abuse by a male or female perpetrator. *Journal of Traumatic Stress Disorders and Treatment, 3*(3): 1–5. http://dx.doi.org/10.4172/2324-8947.1000128

Gill, C. (1973). The sexual episodes in the Satyricon. *Classical Philology, 68*(3): 172–185.

Giugliano, J. (2006). Out of control sexual behavior: A qualitative investigation. *Sexual Addiction and Compulsivity, 13*: 361–375.

Glasser, M. (1979). Some aspects of the role of aggression in the perversions. In: I. Rosen (Ed.), Sexual Deviation (pp. 278–305). Oxford: Oxford University Press.

Glasser, M. (1987). Psychodynamic aspects of paedophilia. *Psychoanalytic Psychotherapy, 3*: 121–135.

Glasser, M., Kolvin, I., Campbell, D., Glasser, A., Leitch, I., & Farrelly, S. (2001). Cycle of child sexual abuse: Links between being a victim and becoming a perpetrator. *British Journal of Psychiatry, 179*: 482–494.

Gleaves, D. H. (1996). The sociocognitive model of dissociative identity disorder: A reexamination of the evidence. *Psychological Bulletin, 120*(1): 42–59.

Glover, E., & Brierley, M. (1940). An investigation of the technique of psycho-analysis. Oxford: Williams & Wilkins.

Goldner, V. (1991). Toward a critical relational theory of gender. *Psychoanalytic Dialogues, 1*: 249–272.

Goodman, A. (1992). Sexual addiction: Designation and treatment. *Journal of Sex and Marital Therapy, 18*: 303–314.

Goodsitt, A. (1985). Eating disorders: A self-psychological perspective. In: D. M. Garner & P. E. Garfinkel (Eds), *Handbook of Psychotherapy for Anorexia Nervosa and Bulimia* (pp. 55–82). New York: Guilford.

Gorey, K. M., & Leslie, D. R. (1997). The prevalence of child sexual abuse: Integrative review adjustment for potential response and measurement biases. *Child Abuse and Neglect, 21*: 391–398.

Groth, A. N. (1979). *Men Who Rape: The Psychology of the Offender*. New York: Plenum.

Gull, W. W. (1874). Anorexia nervosa (apepsia hysterica, anorexia hysterica). *Clinical Society's Transactions*, *7*: 22.

Gupta, G. R. (2000). Gender, sexuality, and HIV/AIDS: The what, the why, and the how. *Canadian HIV/AIDS Policy Law Review*, *5*: 86–93.

Gwandure, C. (2007). Sexual assault in childhood: Risk HIV and AIDS behaviours in adulthood. *AIDS Care*, *19*: 1313–1315.

Hakeem, A. (2010). Deconstructing gender in trans-gender identities. *Group Analysis*, *43*: 141–154.

Hakeem, A. (2012). Psychotherapy for gender identity disorders. *Advances in Psychiatric Treatment*, *18*(1): 17–24.

Hanson, R. F., Kievit, L. W., Saunders, B. E., Smith, D. W., Kilpatrick, D. G., Resnick, H. S., & Ruggiero, K. J. (2003). Correlates of adolescent reports of sexual assault: Findings from the National Survey of Adolescents. *Child Maltreatment*, *8*: 261–272.

Harrington, M. (1962). *The Other America*. London: Macmillan.

Harris, A. (2002). Gender as contradiction. In: M. Dimen & V. Goldner (Eds), *Gender in Psychoanalytic Space: Between Clinic and Culture* (pp. 91–115). New York: Other.

Hart, O. v. d., & Steele, K. (1997). Time distortions in dissociative identity disorder: Janetian concepts and treatment. *Dissociation*, *10*: 91–103.

Hatfield, E. (1988). Passionate and compassionate love. In: R. Sternberg and M. Barns (Eds), The Psychology of Love (pp. 191–217). New Haven, CT: Yale University Press.

Haworth-Hoeppner, S. (2000). The critical shapes of body image: The role of culture and family in the production of eating disorders. *Journal of Marriage and Family*, *62*: 212–227.

Hayes, S., & Carpenter, B. (2013). Social moralities and discursive constructions of female sex offenders. *Sexualities*, *16*: 159–179.

Hellerstein, D., Aviram, R., & Kotov, K. (2004). Beyond "handholding": Supportive therapy for patients with BPD and self-injurious behavior. *Psychiatric Times*, *21*(8): 1–2.

Herdt, G. H. (1981). *Guardians of the flutes: Idioms of Masculinity*. New York: McGraw-Hill.

Herman, J. L. (1992). *Trauma and Recovery*. London: Pandora.

Hernandez, P., Gangsei, D., & Engstrom, D. (2007). Vicarious resilience: A new concept in work with those who survive trauma. *Family Process*, *46*: 229–241.

Hetherton, J. (1999). The idealization of women: Its role in the minimization of child sexual abuse by females. *Child Abuse and Neglect*, *23*: 161–174.

Hindmarch, I., ElSohly, M., Gambles, J., & Salamone, S. (2001). Forensic urinalysis of drug use in cases of alleged sexual assault. *Journal of Clinical Forensic Medicine, 8*: 197–205.

Hoff, L. A., Hallisey, B. J., & Hoff, M. (2009). *People in Crisis: Clinical and Diversity Perspectives* (6th edition). Oxon: Taylor & Francis.

Holmes, G. R., Offen, L., & Waller, G. (1997). See no evil, hear no evil, speak no evil: Why do relatively few male victims of childhood sexual abuse receive help for abuse-related issues in adulthood? *Clinical Psychology Review, 17*: 69–88.

Hopper, E. (2003). *Traumatic Experience in the Unconscious Life of Groups: The Fourth Basic Assumption: Incohesion: Aggregation/Massification or (ba) I: A/M*. London: Jessica Kingsley.

Hornor, G. (2010). Child sexual abuse: Consequences and implications. *Journal of Pediatric Health Care, 24*: 358–364.

Howell, E. F. (2014). Ferenczi's concept of identification with the aggressor: Understanding dissociative structure with interacting victim and abuser self-states. *The American Journal of Psychoanalysis, 74*: 48–59.

Hudson, J. I., Hiripi, E., Pope, H. G., & Kessler, R. C. (2007). The prevalence and correlates of eating disorders in the National Comorbidity Survey Replication. *Biological Psychiatry, 61*: 348–358.

Huebner, H. F. (1993). *Endorphins, Eating Disorders and Other Addictive Behaviours*. New York: W. W. Norton.

Jacob, C. M. A., & Veach, P. M. (2005). Intrapersonal and familial effects of child sexual abuse on female partners of male survivors. Journal of Counseling Psychology, *52*(3): 284–297.

Jacobs, D. F. (1986). A general theory of addictions: A new theoretical model. *Journal of Gambling Behavior, 2*(1): 15-–31.

Jacobson, E. (1954). Transference problems in the psychoanalytic treatment of severely depressive patients. *Journal of the American Psychoanalytic Association, 2*: 595–620.

Janoff-Bulman, R. (1992). *Shattered Assumptions*. New York: Simon and Schuster.

Joffe, H. (1999). *Risk and "the Other"*. Cambridge: Cambridge University Press.

Joffe, W., & Sandler, J. (1964). Notes on pain, depression, and individuation. *The Psychoanalytic Study of the Child, 20*: 394–424.

Johnson, K., Asher, J., Rosborough, S., Raja, A., Panjabi, R., Beadling, C., & Lawrey, L. (2008). Association of combatant status and sexual violence with health and mental health outcomes in postconflict Liberia. *Journal of the American Medical Association, 300*: 676–690.

Johnson, K., Scott, J., Rughita, B., Kisielewski, M., Asher, J., Ong, R., & Lawry, L. (2010). Association of sexual violence and human rights violations with physical and mental health in territories of the Eastern Democratic Republic of the Congo. *Journal of the American Medical* Association, *304*: 553–562.

Joiner, T. E., Sachs-Ericsson, N. J., Wingate, L. R., Brown, J. S., Anestis, M. D., & Selby, E. A. (2007). Childhood physical and sexual abuse and lifetime number of suicide attempts: A persistent and theoretically important relationship. *Behaviour Research and Therapy, 45*: 539–547.

Jones, A. R., & Fay, G. R. (2004). *Investigation of Intelligence Activities at Abu Ghraib*. Arlington, VA: Department of Defense.

Jones, W., & Morgan, J. (2010). Eating disorders in men: A review of the literature. *Journal of Public Mental Health, 9*(2): 23–31.

Jones, W. R., & Morgan, J. F. (2012). Eructophilia in bulimia nervosa: A clinical feature. *International Journal of Eating Disorders, 45*: 298–301.

Joseph, B. (1982). Addiction to near-death. *International Journal of Psychoanalysis, 63*: 449–456.

Kadambi, M. A., & Ennis, L. (2004). Reconsidering vicarious trauma. *Journal of Trauma Practice, 3*(2): 1–21.

Kahr, B. (2007a). The infanticidal attachment. *Attachment: New Directions in Relational Psychoanalysis and Psychotherapy, 1*: 117–132.

Kahr, B. (2007b). *Sex and the Psyche*. London: Allen Lane.

Kalichman, S. C., Sikkema, K. J., DiFonzo, K., Luke, W. & Austin, J. (2002). Emotional adjustment in survivors of sexual assault living with HIV-AIDS. *Journal of Traumatic Stress, 15*: 289–296.

Kaminski, P. L., Chapman, B. P., Haynes, S. D., & Own, L. (2005). Body image, eating behaviors, and attitudes toward exercise among gay and straight men. *Eating Behaviors, 6*: 179–187.

Kenagy, G. P. (2005). The health and social service needs of transgender people in Philadelphia. *International Journal of Transgenderism, 8*: 49–56.

Keogh, T. (2011). *The Internal World of the Juvenile Sex Offender: Through a Glass Darkly Then Face to Face*. London: Karnac.

Kernberg, O. F. (1993). *Severe Personality Disorders: Psychotherapeutic Strategies*. New Haven, CT: Yale University Press.

Kernberg, O. F. (2008). The destruction of time in pathological narcissism. *International Journal of Psychoanalysis, 89*: 299–312.

Khan, M. (1981). The evil hand: From cumulative traumata to self-control (Trans. Michelle T. Van Khai). *Nouvelle Revue de Psychanalyse, 24*: 5–51.

Kim, K., Trickett, P. K., & Putnam, F. W. (2010). Childhood experiences of sexual abuse and later parenting practices among non-offending mothers of sexually abused and comparison girls. *Child Abuse and Neglect, 34*(8): 610–622.

Kimerling, R., Ouimette, P., & Wolfe, J. (2002). *Gender and PTSD*. New York: Guilford.

Kishur, G., & Figley, C. (1987). *The Relationship between Psychiatric Symptoms of Crime Victims and Their Supporters: Evidence of the Chiasmal Effects of Covictimization*. West Lafayette, IN: Purdue University.

Kitson, C. (2012). Motivation to change. In: J. Fox & K. Goss (Eds), *Eating and Its Disorders* (pp. 75–101). London: John Wiley & Sons.

Klein, M. (1940). Mourning and its relation to manic-depressive states. *The Writings of Melanie Klein. Vol. 1: Love, Guilt and Reparation and Other Works 1921–1945* (pp. 344–369). London: Hogarth, 1975.

Kluft, R. P. (1984a). Aspects in the treatment of multiple personality disorder. *Psychiatric Annals, 14*(1): 51–55.

Kluft, R. P. (1984b). Treatment of multiple personality disorder: A study of 33 cases. *Psychiatric Clinics of North America, 7*: 90–129.

Kohut, H. (1971). *The Analysis of the Self: A Systematic Approach to the Psychoanalytic Treatment of Narcisstic Personality Disorders*. Madison, WI: International Universities Press.

Kohut, H. (1977). *The Restoration of the Self*. New York: International Universities Press.

Kolassa, I.-T., Ertl, V., Eckart, C., Kolassa, S., Onyut, L. P., & Elbert, T. (2010). Spontaneous remission from PTSD depends on the number of traumatic event types experienced. *Psychological Trauma: Theory, Research, Practice, and Policy, 2*: 169–174.

Krafft-Ebbing, R. (1886). *Psychopathia Sexualis*. New York: Paperback Library.

Krahe, B., Temkin, J., Bieneck, S., & Berger, A. (2008). Prospective lawyers' rape stereotypes and schematic decision making about rape cases. Psychology, Crime and Law, *14*: 461–479.

Labbé, J. (2005). Ambroise Tardieu: The man and his work on child maltreatment a century before Kempe. *Child Abuse and Neglect, 29*: 311–324.

Laing, R. D. (1960). *The Divided Self*. London: Tavistock.

Laumann, E. O., Paik, A., & Rosen, R. C. (1999). Sexual dysfunction in the United States: Prevalence and predictors. *Journal of the American Medical Association, 281*: 537–544.

Leader, D. (2009). *The New Black: Mourning, Melancholia and Depression*. London: Penguin.

Leifer, M., Kilbane, T., Jacobsen, T., & Grossman, G. (2004a). A three-generational study of transmission of risk for sexual abuse. *Journal of Clinical Child and Adolescent Psychology, 33*: 662–672.

Leifer, M., Kilbane, T., & Kallick, S. (2004b). Vulnerability or resilience to intergenerational sexual abuse: The role of maternal factors. *Child Maltreatment, 9*(1): 78–91.

Leone, J. E., Sedory, E. J., & Gray, K. A. (2005). Recognition and treatment of muscle dysmorphia and related body image disorders. *Journal of Athletic Training*, *40*: 352–359.

Leserman, J. (2005). Sexual abuse history: Prevalence, health effects, mediators, and psychological treatment. *Psychosomatic Medicine*, *67*: 906–915.

Lev, A. I. (2004). *Transgender Emergence: Therapeutic Guidelines for Working with Transgender People and Their Families*. New York: Haworth.

Levesque, R. R. (1994). Sex differences in the experience of child sexual victimization. *Journal of Family Violence*, *9*: 357–369.

Levin, A. P., & Greisberg, S. (2003). Vicarious trauma in attorneys. *Pace Law Review*, *24*: 245–252.

Lew, M. (1988). *Victims No Longer: Men Recovering from Incest and Other Sexual Child Abuse*. New York: Nevraumont.

Lewes, K. (1988). *The Psychoanalytic Theory of Male Homosexuality*. New York: Simon and Schuster.

Lillywhite, R., & Skidmore, P. (2006). Boys are not sexually exploited? A challenge to practitioners. *Child Abuse Review*, *15*: 351–361.

Linehan, M. (1993). *Cognitive-behavioral Treatment of Borderline Personality Disorder*. New York: Guilford.

MacCarthy, B. (1988). Are incest victims hated? *Psychoanalytic Psychotherapy*, *3*: 113–120.

Maltas, C. P., & Shay, J. (1995). Trauma contagion in partners of survivors of childhood sexual abuse. *American Journal of Orthopsychiatry*, *65*(4): 529–539.

Maltz, W. (2002). Treating the sexual intimacy concerns of sexual abuse survivors. *Sexual and Relationship Therapy*, *17*: 321–327.

Margolin, L. (1985). The effects of mother–son incest. *Lifestyles*, *8*: 104–114.

Mariner, J. (2001). *No Escape: Male Rape in US Prisons*. New York: Human Rights Watch.

Masho, S. W., & Alvanzo, A. (2010). Help-seeking behaviors of men sexual assault survivors. *American Journal of Men's Health*, *4*: 237–242.

Mathis, J. L. (1972). *Clear Thinking About Sexual Deviations*. Chicago, IL: Nelson-Hall.

McCann, I. L., & Pearlman, L. A. (1990). Vicarious traumatization: A framework for understanding the psychological effects of working with victims. *Journal of Traumatic Stress*, *3*: 131–149.

McCoy, E. I. (2012). A study of trauma and scapegoating in the context of incohesion: An example from the oil industry. In: E. Hopper (Ed.), *Trauma and Organizations* (pp. 89–110). London: Karnac.

McDougall, J. (1992). *Plea for a Measure of Abnormality*. New York: Brunner/Mazel.

McGinn, T., Casey, S., Purdin S., & Marsh, M. (2004). Reproductive health for conflict-affected people: Policies research and programmes. London: Overseas Development Institute, Humanitarian Practice Network.

Mehta, D., Klengel, T., Conneely, K. N., Smith, A. K., Altmann, A., Pace, T. W., Rex-Haffner, M., Loeschner, A., Gonik, M., Mercer, K. B., Bradley, B., Müller-Myhsok, B., Ressler, K.J., & Binder, E. B. (2013). Childhood maltreatment is associated with distinct genomic and epigenetic profiles in posttraumatic stress disorder. *Proceedings of the National Academy of Sciences, 110*: 8302–8307.

Meloy, J. R. (1992). *The Psychopathic Mind: Origins, Dynamics and Treatment*. Lanham, MD: Rowman & Littlefield.

Mendel, M. P. (1995). *The Male Survivor: The Impact of Sexual Abuse*. Thousand Oaks, CA: Sage.

Mendelson, M. (1974). *Psychoanalytic Concepts of Depression*. London: Spectrum.

Miller, R. M., & Sutherland, K. J. (1999). Partners in healing: Systemic therapy with surivors of sexual abuse and their partners. *Journal of Family Studies, 5*: 113–120.

Minuchin, S., & Fishman, H. (1981). *Techniques of Family Therapy*. Cambridge, MA: Harvard University Press.

Mitchell, D., Hirschman, R., & Nagayama Hall, G. C. (1999). Attributions of victim responsibility, pleasure, and trauma in male rape. *Journal of Sex Research, 36*: 369–373.

Mond, J., Mitchison, D., & Hay, P. (2014). Eating disordered behaviour in men: Prevalence, impairment in quality of life, and implications for prevention and health promotion. In: L. Cohn and R. Lemberg (Ed.), *Current Findings on Males With Eating Disorders* (pp. 195–204). East Sussex: Routledge.

Morgan, J. F., & Arcelus, J. (2009). Body image in gay and straight men: A qualitative study. *European Eating Disorders Review, 17*: 435–443.

Mosse, G. L. (1998). *The Image of Man: The Creation of Modern Masculinity*. Oxford: Oxford University Press.

Motz, A. (2001). *The Psychology of Female Violence: Crimes Against The Body*. Hove & New York: Brunner-Routledge.

Murray, C., Macdonald, S., & Fox, J. (2008). Body satisfaction, eating disorders and suicide ideation in an Internet sample of self-harmers reporting and not reporting childhood sexual abuse. *Psychology, Health and Medicine, 13*: 29–42.

Nasim, R., & Nadan, Y. (2013). Couples therapy with childhood sexual abuse survivors (CSA) and their partners: Establishing a context for witnessing. *Family Process, 52*: 368–377.

Nath, D. (2011). *We'll Show You You're a Woman: Violence and Discrimination Against Black Lesbians and Transgender Men in South Africa*. New York: Human Rights Watch.

Nel, J. A., & Judge, M. (2008). Exploring homophobic victimisation in Gauteng, South Africa: Issues, impacts and responses. *Acta Criminologica, 21*: 19–36.

Nelson, B. S., & Wampler, K. S. (2000). Systemic effects of trauma in clinic couples: An exploratory study of secondary trauma resulting from childhood abuse. *Journal of Marital and Family Therapy, 26*(2): 171–184.

Nelson, B. S., Wangsgaard, S., Yorgason, J., Kessler, M. H., & Carter-Vassol, E. (2002). Single-and dual-trauma couples: Clinical observations of relational characteristics and dynamics. *American Journal of Orthopsychiatry, 72*(1): 58–69.

Nitsun, M. (2002). *The Anti-group: Destructive Forces in the Group and Their Creative Potential*. London: Routledge.

Nowell, C., & Ricciardelli, L. A. (2008). Appearance-based comments, body dissatisfaction and drive for muscularity in males. *Body Image, 5*: 337–345.

Office for National Statistics (2013). *Crime in England and Wales 2012/13: Findings from the British Crime Survey and Police Recorded Crime*. London: ONS.

Ogden, T. (1982). *Projective Identification and Psychotherapeutic Technique*. New York: Aronson.

O'Leary, P. J., & Gould, N. (2010). Exploring coping factors amongst men who were sexually abused in childhood. *British Journal of Social Work, 40*: 2669–2686.

Orbach, S. (1978). *Fat is a Feminist Issue*. London: Paddington.

Orbach, S. (2005). *Hunger Strike: The Anorectic's Struggle as a Metaphor for Our Age*. London: Karnac.

Orbach, S. (2009). *Bodies*. London: Macmillan.

Owen, J., Wong, Y. J., & Rodolfa, E. (2009). Empirical search for psychotherapists' gender competence in psychotherapy. *Psychotherapy: Theory, Research, Practice, Training, 46*: 448–458.

Papadopoulos, R. K. (2002). "But how can I help if I don't know?" Supervising work with refugee families. In: D. Campbell and B. Mason (Eds), *Perspectives on Supervision* (pp. 157–180). London: Karnac.

Paredes, M., Leifer, M., & Kilbane, T. (2001). Maternal variables related to sexually abused children's functioning. *Child Abuse and Neglect, 25*: 1159–1176.

Parsons, T. (1954). The incest taboo in relation to social structure and the socialization of the child. *The British Journal of Sociology, 5*: 101–117.

Pavlakis, D. (2014). Reputation and the sexual abuse of boys: Changing norms in late-nineteenth-century Britain. *Men and Masculinities, 17*(3): 325–346.

Pearlman, L. A., & Saakvitne, K. W. (1995a). *Trauma and the Therapist: Countertransference and Vicarious Traumatization in Psychotherapy with Incest Survivors*. New York: W. W. Norton.

Pearlman, L. A., & Saakvitne, K. W. (1995b). Treating therapists with vicarious traumatization and secondary traumatic stress disorders. *Compassion Fatigue*. *23*: 150–177.

Peel, M., Mahtani, A., Hinshelwood, G., & Forrest, D. (2000). The sexual abuse of men in detention in Sri Lanka. *The Lancet*, *355*: 2069–2070.

Pereda, N., Guilera, G., Forns, M. & Gómez-Benito, J. (2009). The prevalence of child sexual abuse in community and student samples: A meta-analysis. *Clinical Psychology Review*, *29*: 328–338.

Perilloux, C., Duntley, J. D., & Buss, D. M. (2012). The costs of rape. Archives of *Sexual Behavior*, *41*: 1099–1106.

Petersen, S., & Benishek, L. A. (2001). Social construction of illness: Addressing the impact of cancer on women in therapy. *Women and Therapy*, *23*: 75–100.

Peterson, Z. D., Voller, E. K., Polusny, M. A., & Murdoch, M. (2011). Prevalence and consequences of adult sexual assault of men: Review of empirical findings and state of the literature. *Clinical Psychology Review*, *31*(1): 1–24.

Phang, S. E. (2001). *The Marriage of Roman Soldiers (13 BC–AD 235): Law and Family in the Imperial Army*. Columbia: Brill Academic.

Pine, F. (1984). The interpretive moment: Variations on classical themes. *Bulletin of the Menninger Clinic*, *48*: 54–71.

Pines, M. (1984). Reflections on mirroring. *International Review of Psychoanalysis*, *11*(1): 27–42.

Pinsker, H. (2014). *A Primer of Supportive Psychotherapy*. Oxon: Routledge.

Ponton, L., & Goldstein, D. (2004). Sexual abuse of boys by clergy. *Adolescent Psychiatry*, *28*: 209–229.

Pope, C. G., Menard, W., Pope, H. G., Fay, C., Olivardia, R., & Phillips, K. A. (2005). Clinical features of muscle dysmorphia among males with body dysmorphic disorder. *Body Image*, *2*: 395–400.

Radford, L., Corral, S., Bradley, C., Fisher, H., Bassett, C., Howat, N., & Collishaw, S. (2011). *Child Abuse and Neglect in the UK Today*. London: NSPCC. Available at: http://clok.uclan.ac.uk/6022/ (accessed April 2014).

Rado, S. (1951). Psychodynamic understanding of depression. *Psychosomatic Medicine*, *13*: 51–55.

Rado, S. (1957). Narcotic bondage: A general theory of the dependence on narcotic drugs. *American Journal of Psychiatry*, *114*: 165–170.

Ratican, K. L. (1992). Sexual abuse survivors: Identifying symptoms and special treatment considerations. *Journal of Counseling and Development*, *71*(1): 33–38.

Raudenbush, B., & Zellner, D. (1997). Nobody's satisfied: Effects of abnormal eating behaviors and actual and perceived weight status on body image satisfaction in males and females. *Journal of Social Psychology and Clinical Counseling*, *16*: 95–110.

Read, J., Bentall, R. P., & Fosse, R. (2009). Time to abandon the bio-bio-bio model of psychosis: Exploring the epigenetic and psychological mechanisms by which adverse life events lead to psychotic symptoms. *Epidemiologia e psichiatria sociale*, *18*: 299–310.

Reed, R. C., & Blaine, D. A. (1988). Sexual addictions. *Holistic Nursing Practice*, *2*(4): 75–83.

Reinders, A., Nijenhuis, E., Paans, A., Korf, J., Willemsen, A., & Den Boer, J. (2003). One brain, two selves. *Neuroimage*, *2*: 2119–2125.

Remer., R, & Elliott, J. E. (1988). Characteristics of secondary victims of sexual assault. *International Journal of Family Psychiatry*, *9*: 373–387.

Ricciardelli, L. A., & McCabe, M. P. (2004). A biopsychosocial model of disordered eating and the pursuit of muscularity in adolescent boys. *Psychological Bulletin*, *130*(2): 179–205.

Robertson, J. E. (2002). A clean heart and an empty head: The Supreme Court and sexual terrorism in prison. *North Carolina Law Review*, *81*: 434–482.

Romano, E., & De Luca, R. V. (2001). Male sexual abuse: A review of effects, abuse characteristics, and links with later psychological functioning. *Aggression and Violent Behavior*, *6*: 55–78.

Rørtveit, K., Åström, S., & Severinsson, E. (2009). The feeling of being trapped in and ashamed of one's own body: A qualitative study of women who suffer from eating difficulties. *International Journal of Mental Health Nursing*, *18*: 91–99.

Rosenfeld, H. (1987). Impasse and Interpretation: Therapeutic and Anti-therapeutic Factors in the Psychoanalytic Treatment of Psychotic, Borderline, and Neurotic Patients. London: Routledge.

Ross, C. A., Keyes, B. B., Yan, H., Wang, Z., Zou, Z., Xu, Y., Chen, J., Zhang, H., & Xiao, Z. (2008). A cross-cultural test of the trauma model of dissociation. *Journal of Trauma and Dissociation*, *9*(1): 35–49.

Rothstein, A. (1982). The implications of early psychopathology for the analyzability of narcissistic personality disorders. *International Journal of Psychoanalysis*, *63*: 177–188.

Rubenstein, D., & Sorrentino, D. (2007). Psychotherapy with HIV/AIDS patients: Assessment and treatment plan development. *American Journal of Psychotherapy*, *62*: 365–375.

Rubin, G. (1984). Thinking Sex: Notes for a radical theory of the politics of sexuality. In: C. S. Vance (Ed.), *Pleasure and Danger: Exploring female sexuality* (pp. 3–44). London: Routledge and Kegan Paul.

Rumstein-McKean, O., & Hunsley, J. (2001). Interpersonal and family functioning of female survivors of childhood sexual abuse. *Clinical Psychology Review, 21*: 471–490.

Runtz, M. G., & Schallow, J. R. (1997). Social support and coping strategies as mediators of adult adjustment following childhood maltreatment. *Child Abuse & Neglect, 21*: 211–226.

Sachs, A., & Galton, G. (Eds), (2008). *Forensic Aspects of Dissociative Identity Disorder*. London: Karnac.

Salter, D., McMillan, D., Richards, M., Talbot, T., Hodges, J., Bentovim, A., Hastings, R., Stevenson, J., & Skuse, D. (2003). Development of sexually abusive behaviour in sexually victimised males: a longitudinal study. *The Lancet, 361*: 471–476.

Samuels, E., Khalife, S., Alfonso, A. A., Alvarez, R., & Cohen, M. A. (2011). Early childhood trauma, posttraumatic stress disorder, and non-adherence in persons with AIDS: A psychodynamic perspective. *The Journal of the American Academy of Psychoanalysis and Dynamic Psychiatry, 39*: 633–650.

Scarce, M. (2001). Male on Male Rape: The Hidden Toll of Stigma and Shame. New York: Basic.

Schachtel, E. G. (1959). *Metamorphosis*. New York: Basic.

Schauben, L. J., & Frazier, P. A. (1995). Vicarious trauma: The effects on female counselors of working with sexual violence survivors. *Psychology of Women Quarterly, 19*(1): 49–64.

Schaverien, J. (2003). *Desire and the Female Therapist: Engendered Gazes in Psychotherapy and at Therapy*. East Sussex: Routledge.

Schaverien, J. (2011). Boarding school syndrome: Broken attachments a hidden trauma. *British Journal of Psychotherapy, 27*: 138–155.

Schaverien, J. (2015). *Boarding School Syndrome: The Psychological Trauma of the "privileged" Child*. East Sussex: Routledge.

Scott-Ham, M., & Burton, F. C. (2005). Toxicological findings in cases of alleged drug-facilitated sexual assault in the United Kingdom over a 3-year period. *Journal of Clinical Forensic Medicine, 12*: 175–186.

Senn, T. E., Carey, M. P., & Vanable, P. A. (2008). Childhood and adolescent sexual abuse and subsequent sexual risk behavior: Evidence from controlled studies, methodological critique, and suggestions for research. *Clinical Psychology Review, 28*: 711–735.

Sepler, F. (1990). Victim advocacy and young male victims of sexual abuse: An evolutionary model. In: M. Hunter (Ed.), *The Sexually Abused Male: Volume 1* (pp. 73–86). New York: Lexington.

Shaw, S. (2010). *Report on Violent and Sexual Assaults in Prisons*. London: Howard League for Penal Reform.

Siegel, J. (2008). Splitting as a focus of couples treatment. *Journal of Contemporary Psychotherapy, 38*: 161–168.

Silverman, J. A. (1990). Anorexia nervosa in the male: Early historical cases. In: A. E. Andersen (Ed.), *Males with Eating Disorders* (pp. 3–9). London: Brunner-Routledge.

Sinason, V. (1994). *Treating Survivors of Satanist Abuse*. East Sussex: Routledge.

Sinason, V. (2002). *Attachment, Trauma and Multiplicity: Working with Dissociative Identity Disorder*. East Sussex: Brunner-Routledge.

Sinason, V. (2009). Commentary on paper by Debra Rothschild. *Psychoanalytic Dialogues, 19*: 204–214.

Sivakumaran, S. (2005). Male/male rape and the "taint" of homosexuality. *Human Rights Quarterly, 27*: 1274–1306.

Sivakumaran, S. (2007). Sexual violence against men in armed conflict. *European Journal of International Law, 18*: 253–276.

Slaughter, L. (2000). Involvement of drugs in sexual assault. *The Journal of Reproductive Medicine, 45*(5): 425–430.

Sontag, S. (1989). *AIDS and Its Metaphors*. London: Penguin.

Sorsoli, L., Kia-Keating, M., & Grossman, F. K. (2008). "I keep that hush-hush": Male survivors of sexual abuse and the challenges of disclosure. *Journal of Counseling Psychology, 55*: 333–345.

Southgate, J. (2002). A theoretical framework for understanding multiplicity and dissociation. In: V. Sinason (Ed.), *Attachment, Trauma and Multiplicity: Working with Dissociative Identity Disorder* (pp. 86–106). East Sussex: Routledge.

Spanos, N. P. (1994). Multiple identity enactments and multiple personality disorder: A sociocognitive perspective. *Psychological Bulletin, 116*: 143–165.

Spataro, J., Mullen, P. E., Burgess, P. M., Wells, D. L, & Moss, S. A. (2004). Impact of child sexual abuse on mental health: Prospective study in males and females. *The British Journal of Psychiatry, 184*: 416–421.

Spitz, R. A., & Wolf, K. M. (1946). Anaclitic depression: An inquiry into the genesis of psychiatric conditions in early childhood, II. *The Psychoanalytic Study of the Child, 2*: 313–341.

Steiner, J. (2004). *Psychic Retreats: Pathological Organizations in Psychotic, Neurotic and Borderline Patients*. London: Routledge.

Steiner, J. (2005). The conflict between mourning and melancholia. *Psychoanalytic Quarterly, 74*: 83–104.

Steinhausen, H.-C. (2002). The outcome of anorexia nervosa in the 20th century. *American Journal of Psychiatry, 159*: 1284–1293.

Stemple, L. (2008). Male rape and human rights. *Hastings Law Journal, 60*: 605–647.

Stern, D. B. (2013). *Unformulated Experience: From Dissociation to Imagination in Psychoanalysis*. London: Routledge.

Stewart, M. W., Dobbin, S. A., & Gatowski, S. I. (1996). "Real rapes" and "real victims": The shared reliance on common cultural definitions of rape. *Feminist Legal Studies, 4*: 159–177.

Stoller, R. (1975). *Perversion: The Erotic Form of Hatred*. New York: Random House.

Storr, W. (2011). The rape of men: The darkest secret of War. *The Guardian*. Available at: www.theguardian.com/society/2011/jul/17/the-rape-of-men (accessed April 2016).

Strean, H. S. (2014). *Resolving Counterresistances in Psychotherapy*. New York: Routledge.

Strother, E., Lemberg, R., Stanford, S. C., & Turberville, D. (2012). Eating disorders in men: Underdiagnosed, undertreated, and misunderstood. *Eating Disorders, 20*: 346–355.

Summit, R. (1983). The child sexual abuse accommodation syndrome. *Child Abuse and Neglect, 7*: 177–193.

Tang, S. S. S., Freyd, J. J., & Wang, M. (2008). What do we know about gender in the disclosure of child sexual abuse? *Journal of Psychological Trauma, 6*(4): 1–26.

Tardif, M., Auclair, N., Jacob, M., & Carpentier, J. (2005). Sexual abuse perpetrated by adult and juvenile females: An ultimate attempt to resolve a conflict associated with maternal identity. *Child Abuse & Neglect, 29*: 153–167.

Tehrani, N. (Ed.), (2011). *Managing Trauma in the Workplace: Supporting Workers and Organisations. London*: Routledge.

Terry, K. J. (2008). Stained glass: The nature and scope of child sexual abuse in the Catholic Church. *Criminal Justice and Behavior, 35*: 549–569.

Terry, K. J., Giotakos, O., Tsiliakou, M., & Ackerman, A. R. (2010). Sex offenders: Rape and child sexual abuse. In: C. J. Ferguson (Ed.), *Violent Crime: Clinical and Social Implications* (pp. 229–256). Thousand Oaks, CA: Sage.

Tremblay, G., & Turcotte, P. (2005). Gender identity construction and sexual orientation in sexually abused males. *International Journal of Men's Health, 4*: 131–147.

Tsai, G. E., Condie, D., Wu, M. -T., & Chang, I. -W. (1999). Functional magnetic resonance imaging of personality switches in a woman with dissociative identity disorder. *Harvard Review of Psychiatry, 7*: 119–122.

Van der Kolk, B. A. (1989). The compulsion to repeat the trauma. *Psychiatric Clinics of North America, 12*: 389–411.

Van der Kolk, B. A., McFarlane, A. C., & van der Hart, O. (1996). A general approach to treatment of posttraumatic stress disorder. In: B. A. van der Kolk, A. C. McFarlane & L. Weisaeth (Eds), *Traumatic Stress: The Effects of Overwhelming Experience on Mind, Body, and Society* (pp. 417–440). New York: Guilford.

VanDeusen, K. M., & Way, I. (2006). Vicarious trauma: An exploratory study of the impact of providing sexual abuse treatment on clinicians' trust and intimacy. *Journal of Child Sexual Abuse, 15*(1): 69–85.

Verhaeghe, P. (2008). *On Being Normal and Other Disorders: A Manual for Clinical Psychodiagnostics*. London: Karnac.

Vermetten, E., Schmahl, C., Lindner, S., Loewenstein, R. J., & Bremner, J. D. (2006). Hippocampal and amygdalar volumes in dissociative identity disorder. *American Journal of Psychiatry, 163*: 630–636.

Walsh, A. (1995). Parental attachment, drug use, and facultative sexual strategies. *Social Biology, 42*: 95–107.

Wasco, S. M. (2003). Conceptualizing the harm done by rape applications of trauma theory to experiences of sexual assault. *Trauma, Violence, and Abuse, 4*: 309–322.

Watkins, B., & Bentovim, A. (1992). The sexual abuse of male children and adolescents: A review of current research. *Journal of Child Psychology and Psychiatry, 33*: 197–248.

Weigert, E. (1967). Narcissism: benign and malignant forms. In: R. W. Gibson (Ed.), *Crosscurrents in Psychiatry and Psychoanalysis* (pp. 222–228). Philadelphia, PA: Lippincott.

Welldon, E. V. (1988). *Mother, Madonna, Whore: The Idealisation and Denigration of Motherhood*. London: Karnac.

Welldon, E. V. (1993). Forensic psychotherapy and group analysis. *Group Analysis, 26*: 487–502.

Welldon, E. V. (1996a). Contrasts in male and female sexual perversions. In: C. Cordess & M. Cox (Eds), *Forensic Psychotherapy: Crime, Psychodynamics and the Offender Patient: Volume 2* (pp. 273–289). London: Jessica Kingsley.

Welldon, E. V. (1996b). Group-analytic psychotherapy in an out-patient setting. In: C. Cordess & M. Cox (Eds), *Forensic Psychotherapy: Crime, Psychodynamics and the Offender Patient* (pp. 63–82). London: Jessica Kingsley.

Welldon, E. V. (2011). *Playing with Dynamite: A Personal Approach to the Psychoanalytic Understanding of Perversions, Violence, and Criminality*. London: Karnac.

Wenninger, K., & Heiman, J. R. (1998). Relating body image to psychological and sexual functioning in child sexual abuse survivors. *Journal of Traumatic Stress, 11*: 543–562.

Whiffen, V. E., Judd, M. E., & Aube, J. A. (1999). Intimate relationships moderate the association between childhood sexual abuse and depression. *Journal of Interpersonal Violence, 14*: 940–954.

Whitehead, S., & Barrett, F. (2002). *The Masculinities Reader*. Cambridge: Polity.

Widom, C. S., DuMont, K., & Czaja, S. J. (2007). A prospective investigation of major depressive disorder and comorbidity in abused and neglected children grown up. *Archives of General Psychiatry, 64*(1): 49–56.

Wiersma, N. S. (2003). Partner awareness regarding the adult sequelae of childhood sexual abuse for primary and secondary survivors. *Journal of Marital and Family Therapy, 29*: 151–164.

Wilson, J. P., & Lindy, J. D. (2013). *Trauma, Culture, and Metaphor: Pathways of Transformation and Integration*. London: Taylor & Francis.

Wilson, J. P., Lindy, J. D., & Raphael, B. (1994). Empathic strain and therapist defense: Type I and II CTRs. In: J. P. Wilson & J. D. Lindy (Eds), *Countertransference in the Treatment of PTSD* (pp. 31–61). London: Guilford.

Winnicott, D. W. (1949). Hate in the counter-transference. *International Journal of Psychoanalysis, 30*: 69–74.

Winnicott, D. W. (1953). Transitional objects and transitional phenomena. *International Journal of Psychoanalysis, 34*: 89–97.

Winnicott, D. W. (1960). The theory of the parent–infant relationship. *International Journal of Psychoanalysis, 41*: 585–595.

Winnicott, D. W. (1965). Ego distortion in terms of true and false self. In: *The Maturational Process and the Facilitating Environment: Studies in the Theory of Emotional Development* (pp. 140–152). New York: International Universities Press.

Winnicott, D. W. (1967). *Playing and Reality*. London: Tavistock.

Wolstein, B. (1988). *Essential Papers on Countertransference*. New York: New York University Press.

Wood, B., Orsak, C., Murphy, M., & Cross, H. J. (1996). Semistructured child sexual abuse interviews: Interview and child characteristics related to credibility of disclosure. *Child Abuse & Neglect, 20*(1): 81–92.

Wooden, W. S., & Parker, J. (1982). *Men Behind Bars: Sexual Exploitation in Prison*. New York: Plenum.

Wortis, J. (1954). *Fragments of an Analysis with Freud*. New York: Charter.

Wright, J. (2006). The remains of the day: Transsexuality, psychodynamics and the modern NHS. *Psychoanalytic Psychotherapy, 20*: 140–156.

Zetzel, E. R. (1970). *The Capacity for Emotional Growth*. Oxford: International Universities Press.

Zucker, K. J., & Kuksis, M. (1990). Gender dysphoria and sexual abuse: A case report. *Child Abuse & Neglect, 14*: 281–283.

INDEX